Songs of The Cid

The Epic Poem
The Romances
and the
Carmen Campidoctoris

Translated by
Dan Veach

☙ - STOCKCERO - ❧

© English translation Dan Veach 2022
of this edition © Stockcero 2022

ISBN: 978-1-949938-11-1
Library of Congress Control Number: 2022931949

All rights reserved.
This book may not be reproduced, stored in a retrieval system, or transmitted, in whole or in part, in any form or by any means, electronic, mechanical, photocopying, recording, or otherwise, without written permission of Stockcero, Inc.

Set in Linotype Granjon font family typeface
Printed in the United States of America on acid-free paper.

Published by Stockcero, Inc.
3785 N.W. 82nd Avenue
Doral, FL 33166
USA
stockcero@stockcero.com

Songs of The Cid

The Epic Poem
The Romances
and the
Carmen Campidoctoris

Translated by
Dan Veach

Contents

Introduction vii
This translation xxxv
The Song of The Cid 1
Second Cantar 57
Third Cantar 111
Romances of The Cid 181
The *Carmen Campidoctoris* 233
Notes to *Carmen Campidoctoris* 241
Selected Readings 243

Introduction

This book offers us, for the first time, three different perspectives on Spain's national hero, El Cid. The *Carmen Campidoctoris*, a poem in Latin, is the only surviving work about the Cid that may have been written during his lifetime. *The Song of The Cid*, one of the highlights of world literature, was composed while its hero was still very much in living memory. The *romances* of the Cid are folk ballads that, like today's endless *Star Wars* spinoffs, fill in the gaps with prequels and sequels, adding drama (and, yes, romance) to an already astounding story.

The Song of The Cid and its companions occupy a unique place in the national consciousness of Spain. Imagine that Americans knew George Washington, not through the prosaic accounts of history, but a powerful work of literature that captured the essence of the man and the charisma of his leadership. So it is with Spain and El Cid.

Rodrigo Díaz de Vivar, who came to be known as El Cid, was a humble knight who rose to embody Spain's deepest values and highest aspirations. Offering vision and courage at a time of crisis for Spain and Christendom, he would become the last great hero of epic poetry.

But unlike Achilles or Odysseus, who had long since passed into myth, Rodrigo was a man of flesh and blood, of sober history, closely observed and chronicled by friend and foe alike. Even Ibn Bassam, the Moorish historian, was filled with grudging admiration for his enemy: "This man, who was the scourge of his age, was, by his unflagging and clear-sighted energy, his virile character, and his heroism, a miracle among the great miracles of the Almighty." A man worthy of his myth, Rodrigo Díaz de Vivar bridges the gap between ancient epic and modern history.

The Fall and Rebirth of Christian Spain

Rodrigo lived at a crucial time in Spanish history. When the Roman Empire fell apart, the Visigoths, a powerful tribe of Germanic "barbarians," took possession of Roman Spain. Already converted to Christianity, they ruled with a mixture of Roman and Germanic law. Thus in *The Cid* we find both a "modern" court trial and an ancient trial by combat.

The Visigoths' kingdom ended in civil war and invasion. Spanish ballads tell the tale of a king, Rey Rodrigo, who seduced La Cava, the daughter of Count Julian. The dishonored Count brought in African Moors to help him get revenge.

These "Moors" were armies of Berber tribesmen, fierce North African warriors newly converted to Islam, led by Arabs from the Middle East. Whatever the truth of the Spanish ballads, Moorish troops under Tariq and Musa did cross the straits of Gibraltar in 711, and defeated the Visigothic king Rodrigo. The Rock of Gibraltar is named for one of the conquerors: *Gebel al-Tariq* means "mountain of Tariq" in Arabic.

The Moors went on to conquer almost all of Spain. By the end, only small bands of Christian guerillas and refugees were left, along with indigenous Basques, in the rugged mountains of the north. Slowly and painfully these Christians would struggle back, forming little kingdoms across the peninsula's northern rim. But for now they faced a prosperous, united, and overwhelmingly powerful Moorish Spain.

The Rise of Al-Andalus

The Ummayad Caliph Abd-el-Rahman gathered all of Muslim Spain beneath his rule. There followed a golden age of Islamic culture and civilization, especially in the lushly fertile south, which Muslims still fondly remember as *Al-Andalus*. (To this day, the south of Spain is called *Andalucia*.) The Arab world was far ahead of medieval Europe in science, literature, and civilization. While the West had lost much of its heritage from Greece and Rome, the Arabs eagerly absorbed Greek knowledge from Byzantium and Persia.

Greek learning would inspire a rebirth in Europe a few centuries down the road, but for the Arab world the Renaissance was already in full swing. While Charlemagne could barely read, and never learned to write, the rulers of Al-Andalus vied with their court poets over who could produce the most exquisite verses. Scientists and philosophers were honored, and all the arts of living reached a peak of perfection. This complex and cultivated way of life, reflected in the elegant architecture of the Alhambra, has been remembered ever since as a paradise on earth.

But "paradise" comes from a Persian word meaning "walled garden," and the walls of this exquisite garden at last began to crumble. The Ummayad Caliphate broke up into a number of smaller kingdoms called "taifas," centered around the major cities of southern and central Spain: Seville, Granada, Cordoba, Toledo, Valencia. The competition among these capitals brought culture to even greater heights, but their "walls" were weaker, and they began to give way to the growing strength of the Christian kingdoms in the north.

By the Cid's day, three hundred years after the Moorish conquest, the taifa kingdoms were under the thumb of the new Christian realms: León, Galicia, Navarra, Aragón, and Castile. They were regularly paying tribute (protection money) to King Alfonso and his fellow rulers. The politics of this period were complex and constantly shifting, with Muslim and Christian rulers constantly playing other Christians and Muslims off against each other, with more regard for profit than religion.

The idea that the Christian reconquest of Spain was one long religious crusade is far from the truth. The Italian Popes and the French monks certainly saw it that way, but they were not on the front lines, where Spaniards and Moors were constantly rubbing shoulders, more often in peace than at war: trading, negotiating, and learning from one another for seven hundred years.

Things were never simple in Spain. Some of the Cid's best friends, in real life as in the poem, were Moors—and some of his worst enemies were Spaniards. The few French and Italian attempts to fight a "proper" crusade against the Moors in Spain were fiascos—as witnessed by France's own national epic, the *Song of Roland*.

Rodrigo Díaz of Vivar

Into this fascinating and kaleidoscopic situation was born Rodrigo Díaz of Vivar.
Vivar was a little mill town in Castile, and Rodrigo's family were of the lowest order of nobility, the *infanzones*.

Nobility was based on military service in this age of constant warfare. Anyone with a horse and a sword could be a *caballero*. The word, which came to mean "nobleman or gentleman," originally meant "horseman."

The Cid of the Romances

The popular ballads or *romances* about the Cid have mythologized his childhood with gusto. In sharp contrast to the hero of the epic, who is possessed of supreme self-control, the young Cid is pictured as brash and arrogant, boldly defying the king and even the Pope. Some of these stories, like George Washington's cherry tree, are no doubt too good to be true. But where there's still so much smoke, we may have a young man quick to catch fire.

The ballads tell of a young Rodrigo avenging an insult to his father by killing Count Lozano, the leading noble of King Ferdinand's court. The Count's daughter, Jimena, demands that Ferdinand avenge her father. Summoned to court, Rodrigo arrives "like a wild lion," challenges everyone to combat, and refuses to kiss the king's hand, despite the pleading of his own father.

Things are at an impasse when Jimena proposes an astounding solution: let Rodrigo marry her to resolve the quarrel! Rodrigo agrees, telling Jimena at their wedding, "I killed a man and I give you a man. / Here I am, at your command."

Though not historically attested, the story became a popular one, celebrated in Corneille's *Le Cid*. This early marriage to Jimena Gómez, if it ever took place, is not to be confused with Rodrigo's historically documented marriage, arranged by King Alfonso, to Jimena Díaz, an Austurian noblewoman. The latter is the Doña Jimena (or Ximena) of the epic poem.

The Sons of Ferdinand

We do know for a fact that Rodrigo was raised in King Ferdinand's court. This practice of fostering the children of nobles was common in royal courts. Rodrigo grew up with Sancho, the king's eldest son, and the two became close friends. Rodrigo would serve as Sancho's champion and standard-bearer. But not before the dying King Ferdinand made a disastrous decision, one that would haunt his children, and Rodrigo, the rest of their lives.

After centuries of warfare and diplomacy, most of the kingdoms of Christian Spain were now under Ferdinand's rule. The tables were turned on the fragmented Muslim taifas, now faced with a strong, more united Christian Spain. Sancho expected the kingdom would pass intact to him, as Ferdinand's oldest son. Instead, Ferdinand decided to give each of his sons a kingdom of their own: Castile to Sancho, León to Alfonso, and Galicia to García.

It was a recipe for civil war. Sancho, feeling cheated of his rightful heritage, first joined with Alfonso to overthrow García. Then Sancho defeated Alfonso, reuniting all three kingdoms. Rodrigo played a leading role in these campaigns, at one point rescuing Sancho from capture by Alfonso's forces. The defeated brothers were exiled to their former Moorish tributaries, García to Seville, Alfonso to Toledo.

Sancho now had everything he wanted—except for one minor irritation. Alfonso was in league with his sister Urraca, and, according to the ballads, she still held the city of Zamora. Sancho laid seige to this last pocket of resistance.

Rodrigo and Urraca

The *romances* tell a spicy story about Rodrigo and Urraca. Sancho sends Rodrigo to Urraca to negotiate the surrender of Zamora. Urraca reminds Rodrigo of how they grew up together as children. Then she scolds him for marrying Jimena, when he could have had her—a princess—instead! When Rodrigo returns without her surrender, Sancho accuses him of being in love with Urraca.

Unfortunately for Sancho, another knight *was* in love with Urraca, and willing to do anything for her. Vellido Adolfo slipped out of Zamora and, pretending to be a traitor to Urraca, gained an audience with King Sancho. Seizing his chance, he dealt Sancho a mortal wound with his spear, escaping back to the safety of Zamora.

With one stroke, the hopes of Rodrigo and all the Castilians were crushed. While they accompanied Sancho's body to Castile for burial, Urraca sent Alfonso the glad tidings: he now ruled the kingdom that Sancho gave his life to reunite.

Alfonso and Urraca

There is no doubt that Alfonso and Urraca had a special relationship—whether or not it extended, as rumor said, to incest. The ballads and histories both implicate her in the plot to assassinate Sancho and bring Alfonso to the throne. Returning the favor, Alfonso named Urraca as his queen, even though she was his sister, not his wife. Oddly enough, a charter signed by Alfonso states that Sancho "was killed on the orders of Doña Urraca, his sister." (*fuit occisus per consilium domna Urraca, germana sua.* Pidal, p. 111.) A shocking thing to admit officially—perhaps he neglected to read the fine print.

Urraca's prayer book also contains this interesting *mea culpa*: "I, Urraca, a miserable sinner, do confess to all the sins I have committed through pride, in thought, word, and deed, of *incest, murder*, perjury...." (Pidal, p. 123. Italics mine.) Not the usual sins a lady would bring to confession, to say the least.

The Oath of Santa Gadea

The reversal of Rodrigo's fortunes was a cruel one. As the champion and friend of Sancho, he could expect but cold comfort at the court of King Alfonso. Alfonso's nobles from León were the top dogs now, and they despised this Castilian upstart with suspect loyalties.

Before he would kiss the new king's hand, Rodrigo and the Castilians insisted that Alfonso swear he had no part in the killing of Sancho. This was their legal right, and Alfonso agreed to take the oath at the Church of Santa Gadea in Burgos. As the surviving leader of the Castilian party, Rodrigo may well have administered the oath himself, just as the ballads say he did. This would hardly have endeared him to Alfonso, nor would the oath's final threat: "If you swear falsely, may it please God that a vassal slay you just as the traitor Vellido Adolfo slew King Sancho." (Pidal, 118) Alfonso, the ballad says, turned pale as he said "Amen.".

Showdown in Seville

Alfonso needed Rodrigo's loyalty to pacify Castile. And so, much as he might have to grit his teeth, he treated his brother's champion with honor and respect. Hoping to reconcile Rodrigo with his Leonese nobility, Alfonso arranged a marriage between Rodrigo and Jimena Díaz, a descendant of the royal family of León. Signing the wedding document were two men who would become Rodrigo's bitter enemies at court: García Ordóñez and Pedro Ansúrez, the Count of Carrión.

When Alfonso sent Rodrigo to Seville to collect the tribute money, his enemies saw their chance. García Ordóñez joined forces with the king of Granada to raid the kingdom of Seville—and also embarrass Rodrigo. When he heard of their attacks, Rodrigo sent a note requesting they desist. Getting a scornful refusal, he set out with a mixed troop of Moors and Christians to stop them. Though outnumbered, he won the battle of Cabra and captured García Ordoñez.

Rodrigo released him quickly, but not (the poem says) before taking this chance to pull García's beard. This was a serious insult to one's masculine honor, and Ordóñez never forgave him for it. He was certainly among those "evil enemies" who advised King Alfonso to exile Rodrigo.

Rodrigo becomes *El Cid*

There are various stories about how Rodrigo acquired the name *El Cid*. It comes from the Arabic *Sidi*, meaning "lord." It was likely a term of respect from the Moors he met both in combat and diplomacy. Moorish slang was common in Christian Spain—in the poem, even King Alfonso addresses Rodrigo by his Moorish nickname.

The Song of The Cid

We come now to the time of Rodrigo's life that is dealt with in the epic poem. *The Song of The Cid* begins with the hero at his lowest point. Rodrigo has been exiled from Castile, in disgrace with King Alfonso. Tears are streaming from his eyes as he looks back one last time on his deserted household.

The first leaf of our manuscript is missing, so we don't know the cause of this exile. Exile was not unusual in Spain, or the medieval world in general. In actual history, the Cid was exiled at least three times during his tempestuous relationship with Alfonso. The king was too quick to believe the slanders of his envious courtiers. Alfonso would pay a terrible price, as we shall see, for this petty jealousy.

"My evil enemies have brought this on me," says the Cid. Perhaps García Ordoñez, still sore about his beard, accused the Cid of stealing Seville's tribute money. At any rate, this is the accusation that seems to have gotten abroad. The Cid, who is actually broke at the start of his exile in the poem, will make clever use of this slander.

As the Cid's faithful followers take to the road, he makes an astounding remark to his right-hand man: "Cheer up, Alvar Fáñez!" he says. "We've just been kicked out of this country!"

One editor tries to explain this by adding a line that's not the poem: "But we shall return in great honor to Castile." But no explanation is needed. Time and again we'll see the Cid taking adversity lightly, even thanking God for sending it his way. This is a glimpse of that irrepressible spirit which made men willing to follow him anywhere.

As the Cid left his estate, a crow crossed his path from the right—a good omen. When he reaches Burgos, however, one flies from the left, or sinister side. Things are indeed bad in Burgos. King Alfonso has forbidden anyone to help the Cid. Every door is locked and barred. Watching the Cid pass by, the citizens exclaim in sorrow: "What a good vassal—if only he had a good lord!" As neat a summary of the poem as one could wish.

At last, in a touching moment, a nine-year-old girl greets the Cid and explains the situation. Only one man in town is courageous enough to help them. Martín Antolínez gives them food and wine, and arranges a loan with two sharp moneylenders, Raquel and Vidas.

The Cid, making use of the accusation against him, offers two "treasure chests" as security for the loan. Aha, the moneylenders think—the stolen treasure from Seville! But the tightly-locked chests are heavy, not with treasure, but with sand.

The Cid deeply regrets this deception, but for now it's

the only way to stay alive. In one of the poem's most delightfully novelistic scenes, Martín and the moneylenders haggle shrewdly over terms and kickbacks for the loan. While other epics would skip such un-heroic details, *The Cid* doesn't flinch from the real life of its time.

These moneylenders, Raquel and Vidas, are likely Jewish, since Christians were not allowed to lend money for interest. ("Raquel" is a Semitic name, and "Vidas" may be a Spanish translation of "*Haim*," the Hebrew word for "life.") Our manuscript of the poem does not mention paying Raquel and Vidas back, but other romances and chronicles do.

Stopping at the monastery of San Pedro, the Cid says goodbye to his wife Ximena and his two daughters, who will stay there. Men seeking their fortunes join him from all over Spain, and together they set off into Moorish lands, to earn their bread by blood and sweat and battle.

The Almoravid invasion

Leaving the poem for a moment, things were looking good for Christian Spain. The Moorish tribute game had grown so profitable that King Alfonso and his peers, having taken back about half of Spain, were no longer focused on conquering Moorish territory. Indeed, they lacked the population to occupy it. Perhaps aware that the taifa kingdoms were more productive in Moorish hands, they were content, for now, to milk them for all they could get.

If the Christians were not exactly Crusaders, the Moorish kings were hardly strict Muslims either, indulging freely in alcohol (forbidden by Islam) and the pleasures of the flesh. They were not alone: King Alfonso's only son was born of Zaida, a Muslim princess of Seville. Things might have gone on in this civilized, slightly decadent manner had not religious fundamentalism, in the form of Almoravid armies, suddenly reared its disapproving head.

King Alfonso, greedy for gold, began to put the squeeze on his Moorish milk cows. To meet his demands, the taifa kings had to impose heavy taxes, in forms not sanctioned by the Quran. This led to unrest and rebellion among their subjects. At last, Mutamid of Seville refused to pay his tribute any longer.

Alfonso promptly besieged the city. It was the last straw. In a replay of the original Moorish conquest, Mutamid and the other taifa kings appealed to Africa for help. They did so with great trepidation. Yúsuf, the king of Morocco, was a strict fundamentalist Muslim. His Almoravid armies were Berber tribesmen, tough and still on fire with religious zeal. The exquisite culture of *Al-Andalus* meant nothing to Yúsuf and his men. Both the Christians and Muslims of Spain were in for a very rude shock.

The Battle of Sagrajas

When Alfonso met Yúsuf at Sagrajas in 1085, the battle was close and hard-fought. At first the Christians had the upper hand, fighting against the troops of the taifa kings. But the tide turned when Yúsuf threw in his Berber infantry, spearmen with tough shields of hippopotamus hide, marching in disciplined formations to the fearful sound of Moorish drums. Next morning the muezzins made their call to prayer atop mountains of Christian heads.

Spain's Moorish taifa kings fared little better. Fed up with their moral laxity and constant bickering, Yúsuf deposed them one by one, until he controlled most of Andalusia. King Mutamid of Seville, who invited Yúsuf over in the first place, repented his choice and allied himself again with King Alfonso. Too late: Seville also fell to the Moroccans.

At Sagrajas and ever after, Alfonso would pay a terrible price for exiling the Cid, Spain's greatest warrior. From that point on, Alfonso would lose every battle with the Moors. The Cid, defending Valencia from these same Almoravides, was victorious every time. Indeed, the Cid was never defeated in battle, by Christians or Moors. A brilliant strategist as well as a powerful warrior, he might well have made the difference at Sagrajas.

Earning one's bread among the Moors

But for now, the Cid's glorious victories at Valencia are far in the future. Only 600 men cross the frontier with him into exile. They must earn their living by raiding Moorish lands, capturing some towns and extracting tribute from others. In the eyes of the Moors, the Cid and his men are no better than bandits, and he admits as much himself:

"Here we are in their country,
doing all kinds of damage,
drinking their wine and eating their bread.
They have every right to besiege us!"

This largeness of spirit, this ability to sympathize with the enemy, is rare indeed, in the Cid's day or ours. Far from excusing himself on religious grounds, the Cid feels empathy toward the Moors, and shows as much mercy as he can. At one point he frees two hundred captives, "that none may speak ill of me." When he defeats a Moorish army at Alcocer, he shares the plunder with its Moorish citizens. The poem says they wept to see him leave, which may seem like a stretch. But clearly the Cid, and his poet, cared about Moorish opinion, and Moorish tears.

In the First *Cantar* (Song) of the poem, filled with realistic and gripping depictions of small-scale warfare, we come to know the Cid on an intimate level: his generosity with foes, his humility and wisdom in council, his cheer and humor in the face of desperate situations.

The Song of The Cid, like the Cid himself, is sober and modest. His band is small, their battles and body counts believable—unlike the vast multitudes in *The Song of Roland*. "We happy few" are witness to the gradual rise of a hero who, starting from nothing, would come to rival kings in glory, and exceed them in honor.

The Second *Cantar*: Triumph and Reconciliation

The Cid's forces grow as the news of his victories spreads through Spain. Valencia, the great Moorish power in the region, watches his rise with concern, until at last they feel compelled to stop him. His struggles with that great city, after three years of "sleeping by day and marching by night," culminate in victory. The high point of *The Cid*, literally and emotionally, comes when he takes his wife and daughters to the top of Valencia's citadel, and shows them the lands he has won for them.

At this point the Cid, master of a great realm of his own, could have declared himself a king. He owed nothing to Alfonso, after all. But, showing remarkable loyalty, the Cid insists he is still Alfonso's vassal. Alfonso, impressed by the Cid's achievements (as well as his generous gifts), ends the Cid's exile and gives him back his estates. Much to the king's embarrassment, the Cid insists on an ancient ritual, getting down on his hands and knees and eating grass as a token of submission.

The Moors, though equally impressed, were not nearly as pleased. As soon as the Cid won Valencia, the king of Seville attacked him with thirty thousand men. Then, after the Cid's wife and daughters had joined him, the Almoravids sent fifty thousand from Morocco. (The poem says they were led by King Yúsuf, but instead he sent one of his generals, reluctant to face the Cid himself.)

Doña Ximena is frightened, but the Cid thanks God that the Moors have come. Now he can show his family how he and his men earn their bread. After the victory, he says "You see this bloody sword and sweating horse? It's with these that we conquer the Moors."

Now that the Cid has won such wealth and fame, Diego and Fernando, the Infantes of Carrión, ask for his daughters in marriage. (*Infante* means noble youth.) Although this is an honor, since they rank far above him, the Cid is not overly pleased with these effete young brothers. Still, eager to please his king, he gives in to Alfonso's pleading on their behalf. The marriage takes place in Valencia, amid jousting and great celebration. The Cid now has everything he wants, it seems, and a fairy tale would end "happily ever after" here.

The Third *Cantar*: The Outrage at Corpes.

But *The Cid* is not a fairy tale. After a pleasant honeymoon, the Infantes Diego and Fernando, the Cid's new sons-in-law, begin to show their true colors. When a pet lion escapes in the palace, both run and hide. The Cid, unfazed, takes the lion by the scruff and puts it back in its pen. The Cid's men poke fun at Diego and Fernando, which they bitterly resent.

The Almoravides, under King Búcar (historically one of Yúsuf's generals, Abu Bekr) attack Valencia again. The Infantes, terrified, avoid the fighting, though they claim to have done great deeds. When the Cid's men continue to laugh at his sons-in-law behind his back, they plot revenge.

The Infantes get the Cid's permission to take his daughters to Carrión. On the way, in the Oak Grove of Corpes, they strip and beat them and leave them for dead, congratulating themselves on their manly deed. The daughters, Elvira and Sol, are rescued by a cousin traveling with them. When the Cid hears of this, he swears—not revenge, but that justice will be done.

At his request, King Alfonso convenes a court in Toledo. The Infantes plot to kill the Cid there. Suspecting as much, the Cid and his men wear chain mail and swords beneath their robes. But Alfonso enforces strict discipline, and the court imposes a heavy fine on the Infantes.

This was justice according to Roman law. But money alone could not atone for such a crime. To recover his honor and avenge his daughters, the Cid now invokes ancient

Germanic law. He demands a trial by combat: the Infantes of Carrión must fight the Cid's men, who challenge them in court. With grand ceremony, King Alfonso presides over this brutal judicial battle, the climax of the poem.

The Cid is vindicated at last, his family's honor cleared. The Princes of Navarra and Aragón ask for the hands of his daughters. A fairy-tale ending at last? Yes, except that it happens to be true. His daughters Cristina and María (Elvira and Sol in the poem) both married royal princes. Cristina gave birth to King García Ramirez of Navarra. García's daughter Blanca (or Blanche) married Sancho III of Castile, giving birth to Alfonso VIII. Fittingly, this great-great-grandson of the Cid ended the last Moorish threat to Spain at the battle of Las Navas de Tolosa. And thus *The Cid*'s last lines, like so much of this remarkable poem, ring true to history:

> *Today his kinsmen are the kings of Spain*
> *and all now share in the honor of the Cid.*

Form and creation of the poem

As with *Beowulf*, only one manuscript of *The Cid* has survived. This manuscript was "written" (or rather copied) by Per Abbat, most likely a monk, in 1207 A.D. Again like *Beowulf*, it has three sections of roughly a thousand lines apiece. The sections, or *Cantares*, are not marked in the manuscript, but the Second *Cantar* starts off with "Here begins the story of the great deeds of the Cid," and ends with "Here the verses of this song come to an end." While these are clearly not the beginning or end of the poem, each *Cantar*, like each section of *Beowulf*, was presumably meant for one night's entertainment.

The poem does not rhyme, and the meter and line lengths are irregular. This "roughshod" rhythm becomes a real delight, making us feel we are riding horseback with the Cid. Where Beowulf relies on alliteration, the repetition of consonants, for its poetic effect, *The Cid* uses assonance: words whose last syllables share the same vowel. The numbers you see throughout the poem correspond to *laises*, sections whose lines end in syllables with identical vowels. There is some logic to these *laises*: often a change in assonance will signal a change in subject.

We know that epic poems like Homer's *Odyssey* were composed in the poet's mind and performed from memory—or perhaps improvised, as jazz musicians do. In fact, the Greeks had no written language in Homer's time. Clearly, poets do not need writing to make great and complex works of art.

One clue to this kind of "oral poetry" is its use of the same phrases over and over, to describe the hero or fill out the rhythm of a line. These stock phrases, like Homer's "rose-fingered dawn," give the poet time to think and help him compose on the fly. We find them in abundance in *The Cid*. Just as Odysseus is the man "skilled in all ways of contending," the Cid is always the man "born in a fortunate hour," or "who girded on his sword in a fortunate hour."

A *writer*, with all the time in the world at his disposal, would say, "How boring! What a cliché! Let's think of a different way to describe him." But the oral poet, performing live before an audience, thinks "Thank goodness! This little phrase I've memorized will just fill that gap. Now I can think about what happens next." The oral poet has his mind on the building he's constructing, and doesn't mind if the bricks look much alike.

One can imagine a natural process in which short folk ballads, telling popular tales of a hero, accumulate over time into an epic. (See the *romances* of the Cid included here.) Unfortunately, we have no evidence of ballads before *The Cid*, which may have appeared within a hundred years of the hero's death. There was a poem actually *written* about him during his lifetime: the *Carmen Campidoctoris*, an unfinished epic in Latin penned by a Catalan monk (also translated here). However, Spain's many *romances* about the Cid, poems certainly meant for oral performance, were all written down many years after the epic, and some seem to be borrowing from it. Or perhaps the poem borrowed from them, in an earlier oral form? We still can't say which was the chicken, which the egg.

Poetry versus History

The Song of The Cid has the *feel* of history—gritty, immediate, finely detailed. And a multitude of those little details, both of people and places, have since been confirmed by historians. Whether writing or composing orally, the poet must have consulted first-hand sources, perhaps some who rode with the Cid themselves.

But the poet was also an artist. He had a story to tell—and there was a definite moral to that story. First of all, as Robert Burns would say, "A man's a man for a' that." Birth and position matter less than personal virtue and courage. The Cid was born of the lowest rank of nobility, in the humble mill town of Vivar. In his trial at court, the Counts of Carrión cast scorn upon his birth, telling the Cid to go back to Vivar and mind his flour mills. But Spain needed real men to face the Moorish threat, not proud but empty titles.

Second, Spain needed unity and loyalty in its time of crisis—which was still ongoing as the poet wrote. The Cid, despite all the injustice done to him, insists on remaining loyal to his king. This is true to history. Fortunately for the poet, he had a *real* hero to work with.

But, as the people of Burgos said, "What a good vassal, if only he had a good lord!" His lord, King Alfonso, would need a drastic makeover. The real Alfonso was petty and vacillating, easily swayed by courtiers jealous of the

Cid. He exiled the hero three times in all, at a terrible cost to Spain. Spain needed a better king—and in the poem it got one. Fooled once by his courtiers into exiling the Cid, the poem's Alfonso sees the error of his ways, graciously forgives the hero, and stands by him loyally ever after. In fact, the Cid and Alfonso *were* reconciled at last, so while the poem does neaten things up, it gets the ending right.

Even more complex than the Cid's dealings with Alfonso was his single greatest achievement: the conquest of Valencia. In the poem it's a single short battle. In reality it was a long and agonizing process, as pro-Cid and pro-Almoravid parties among the Moors struggled to control the city. This conquest spoke as much for the Cid's diplomacy, his tact and regard for Moorish feelings, as it did for his military strength. But few of us have the patience of the Cid, so the poet spares us these exasperating details.

There are other known differences from history. Minaya Alvar Fáñez was a close friend of the Cid, but not his right-hand man in exile. Instead, he was one of Alfonso's generals, and lost every battle he fought with the Almoravides. Though the Cid's daughters are central to the plot, he also had a son, Diego, who died fighting for King Alfonso against the Moors. This rather ruthless omission reminds us the poem is a *story*, not a *history* of the Cid.

The villain García Ordóñez is painted as pure evil. And perhaps he was, in relation to the Cid. But history gives us a more nuanced picture. One of the king's favorite courtiers, García was the guardian of Sancho, Alfonso's only son. He died a hero's death at Uclés, covering young Sancho with his shield as the Almoravides surrounded and overwhelmed them. Grief-stricken, Alfonso himself would die within the year.

But the biggest bone of contention is also the most central to the plot: the betrayal of the Cid's daughters by the Infantes of Carrión. This is the crux of the "virtue versus nobility" theme, as the noble but worthless Infantes attack and abandon the daughters of the Cid, the man of lower birth but greater value. Some deny the historicity of the daughters' weddings to the Infantes, and their brutal assault in the Oak Grove of Corpes. The plot line fits the poet's needs too perfectly, and direct evidence for these events is lacking.

But absence of evidence is not evidence of absence. Menéndez Pidal, the foremost historian of *The Cid*, has discovered two young nobles in Alfonso's court, Diego and Fernando González, whose names appear on charters with the Count of Carrión. Referred to as "sons of a Count," they were the right age to marry the daughters of the Cid. Here, perhaps, we have the Infantes of Carrión.

To this day there's a town called Robledo de Corpes (Oak Grove of Corpes), though any oak grove there is long since gone. It's not far from San Esteban de Gormaz, where the Cid's daughters are taken to recover from their attack. In the poem Diego Téllez, a vassal of Alvar Fáñez, takes care of them there. Pidal also found this Diego Téllez, indeed a vassal of Alvar Fáñez, who was Governor of San Esteban at this very time.

Was the Oak Grove of Corpes a pure invention of the poet, or based on events that were well known at the time? We can't say for sure, but, as historians keep proving, it's never safe to bet against *The Cid*.

This translation

Some translations of *The Cid* use rather archaic language, presumably because the poem is "old." But it wasn't old when it was created; in fact, poetry was the main form of *news* at the time. To deliver this news, I aim for a lean, fast-moving line—we're riding horseback, after all.

Since the poet is quite "cavalier" about line lengths, I've also taken liberties with line breaks now and then, to improve the flow or sense. The same applies to the use of the past or present tense, which alternate freely in the original. Stephen Gilman, my Medieval Spanish professor at Harvard, believed the poet used the present tense to bring events into the foreground, making them more vivid. I've done so myself whenever it seemed effective. Verb tenses had not yet settled down in early Spanish, and one also sees the conditional or subjunctive where we would use the present tense.

The section numbers you see in the poem are not in the manuscript. They are based on the *laises*, groups of lines that end with the same vowel assonance in Spanish. A change in assonance, from "o" to "a" for instance, often signals a change in subject. I've added brief section descriptions for the *laises*, and elsewhere in parentheses, being careful not to spoil the suspense of the story. The numbers in the right margin are the line numbers of the original manuscript. In rare instances the translation may break the lines differently for a better flow.

Ancient manuscripts were typically written without breaks or divisions. The oldest Greek manuscripts don't even have spaces between the words. Gradually over the centuries, aids to reading like punctuation, spaces after words and sentences, stanzas in poetry and paragraphs in prose were adopted. Still, even modern printings of *The Cid* and the *romances* consist of page after page of solid, impenetrable blocks of verbiage. I have let some light and air into these lines, where changes of subject or speaker called for it, to make the poem clearer and more inviting to the reader.

While being as faithful as possible, I also wanted this translation to be *fun*. With a chatty, novelistic poet, despicable villains, terrifying enemies, and a hero who's not afraid to show his human side, I hope you'll find *The Song of The Cid* as enjoyable as I have.

Dan Veach
Atlanta, Georgia
2018

The Song of The Cid

[The first leaf of the manuscript is missing. The following passage in italics has been reconstructed by Menéndez Pidal from Spanish historical chronicles, some of which use the poem as a major source. The Cid has been exiled by King Alfonso; he has nine days to leave Castile. He asks his household troops if they want to go with him.

*"and those who go with me, may God sustain them,
and with those who stay behind, I am content."*

Then Alvar Fáñez, his first cousin, spoke:

*"We will go with you, Cid, through cities and wilderness
and never fail you while our bodies last.
For you we will wear out mules and horses,
our goods and clothes and everything we have.
We will never stop serving you as loyal vassals."*

*Every man agreed with Alvar Fáñez.
The Cid thanked them for what they had said.*

*My Cid set out from Vivar on the road to Burgos,
leaving his home disinherited, desolate.*

Here the manuscript begins:]

1. A LAST LOOK BACK

Tears streaming from his eyes, he turned his head
to look at his old home one more time.
He saw the doors ajar, the gates unlocked
the clothes hooks empty of coats and cloaks
the perches bare of hawks or falcons. 5

He sighed, My Cid, from his heavy load of care
and said in even, measured tones,
"Thanks be to you, our Father in Heaven!
My bitter enemies have brought this on me."

2. OMENS ON THE ROAD

Then they spurred onward, releasing the reins. 10
At the gate of Vivar, the crow flew on their right.
Entering Burgos, it flew on the sinister side.

The Cid shrugged and shook his head.
"Cheer up, Alvar Fáñez," he said.
"We've just been kicked out of this country!"

3. BURGOS

My Cid Ruy Díaz entered Burgos 15
with a company of sixty pennants.
Men and women flocked to see him pass.

The burghers and their wives sat at their windows,
eyes streaming, so great was their sorrow.
From every mouth one thought was heard:
"God, what a good vassal—if only he had a good lord!" 20

4. THE KING'S LETTER. A LITTLE GIRL NINE YEARS OLD.

They would gladly have given him hospitality
but King Alfonso's anger was so great that no one dared.
Last night the king's letter had arrived, all stamped and sealed
forbidding anyone to give the Cid Ruy Díaz
a place to stay. If someone did, in truth 25
he would be stripped of everything he had,
body and soul and even the eyes from his face.
This was a great pain for these Christian people.
They hid themselves from the Cid, none dared to speak. 30

The Campeador rode up to an inn
but found the door securely locked.
For fear of King Alfonso, they all agreed
that unless the Cid broke it down by force
they would not open anything.
The Cid's men shouted out to them, 35
those inside would not reply.
My Cid spurred forward to the door
took his foot from the stirrup and gave it a kick.
The door, locked tight, did not budge.

A little girl, just nine years old, appeared before his eyes.   40
"Campeador, in a good hour you strapped on your sword!
The king has forbidden us from helping you.
Last night his letter came,
strongly stamped and sealed. We do not dare
to open our doors or invite you anywhere
or we will lose our goods and homes   45
and even the eyes from our faces.
Cid, you gain nothing from our harm.
May the Creator watch over you, with all His holy power!"
Having said this, the child returned home.

The Cid could see that the king would have no mercy.   50
He left the inn and spurred through Burgos.
When he came to the Church of Santa María, he dismounted
got down on his knees and prayed with all his heart.
Mounting once more, he passed through the city gate
and crossed the river Arlanzón. Outside of Burgos,   55
on the sandy shore, he dismounted and pitched his tent.

My Cid Ruy Díaz, who strapped on his sword in a fortunate hour,
stayed by the river when no house would let him in.
Around him was a worthy company   60
camping as if they were all in a wilderness.
He was forbidden to buy in Burgos
any kind of food at all. They would not sell him
a single penny's worth.

5. The good man of Burgos

Martín Antolínez, a good man of Burgos   65
brought bread and wine to the Cid and his men.
He did not buy them, but had them in store.
The provisions he gave them were plenty,
the Cid and those who serve him were satisfied.

Martín Antolínez spoke, hear what he said: 70
"Campeador, in a good hour you were born!
Tonight we will lie here, and leave tomorrow.
I will be accused of serving you
and the wrath of King Alfonso will fall upon me.
If we escape alive and well,   75
sooner or later he'll want me for his friend.
If not, I don't give a fig for what I leave behind."

6. The chests of sand

My Cid spoke, who strapped on his sword in a fortunate hour:
"Martín Antolínez, you are a hardy lance!
If I live, I will double your reward.   80
My gold and silver are spent,
as you plainly see
and I must have something to pay my men.

"I hate to do this, but otherwise we have nothing.
With your help I want to make two chests.   85
We'll fill them with sand so they're nice and heavy,
covered with leather and fancy studs.

7.

"The leather should be red, the studs of gold.
Go to Raquel and Vidas for me, secretly.
Tell them I can't buy in Burgos, the king is angry,   90
and I can't carry all my money, it's too heavy.
Tell them I'll pawn it for what they think is right.
And, so that no Christian sees them,
tell them to come at night.
May God and all His saints see what I've done.
I do it because I must, with a heavy heart."   95

8.

Martín Antolínez does not delay.
He heads for Burgos, to the castle,
asking where Raquel and Vidas are.

9. A BARGAIN WITH RAQUEL AND VIDAS

Raquel and Vidas were found together,   100
engaged in counting the money they had gained.
Martín Antolínez approached them cleverly:
"Are you there, Raquel and Vidas, my dear friends?
I would like to speak with you in private."
Without delay, the three withdrew.   105
"Raquel and Vidas, give me both your hands

and swear you won't tell this to Christians or Moors,
for I will make you rich for life. You will never want again.

"When the Campeador was sent to collect the tribute
he received a huge amount of wealth and treasure. 110
He kept a good bit for himself—
for this he was exiled and accused.

"He has two chests full of gleaming gold.
You have seen how he angered the king
and left behind his lands and houses. 115
He cannot keep those chests, they would be discovered.
The Cid wants to leave them in your hands
if you'll lend him some money—whatever you think is right.
Take the chests and keep them safe,
and swear not to look inside them for one whole year." 120

Raquel and Vidas took counsel with one another:
"We have to make a profit on any business.
We know quite well he must have made some money
when he entered Moorish lands and brought back treasure. 125
And a man can't sleep easy who carries a lot of coin.

"We will take the two chests off your hands
and put them in a place they'll never find them.
But tell us, for the Cid, how much he wants
to borrow, and what profit he will give us for this year?" 130
Martín Antolínez answered cleverly:
"My Cid only wants what is fair.
He asks very little to keep his money safe.

Men in need are coming to My Cid from everywhere,
and so he needs from you six hundred marks."   135
Raquel and Vidas say, "We will give it gladly."

"You see that night is coming.
The Cid is in a hurry—
we need those marks right now."

"That's not how business is done," say Raquel and Vidas.
"First comes taking, then comes giving."   140

Martín Antolínez says, "That's fine with me.
Come and meet the famous Campeador
and we will help you, as is only proper,
to take the chests and put them in your keeping
so that neither Moor nor Christian knows about it."   145

Raquel and Vidas say, "That's fine with us.
The chests in hand, we'll pay six hundred marks."

In secret and with a good will
Martín Antolínez rides off with Raquel and Vidas.
He doesn't take the bridge, but fords the river   150
so no one in Burgos will get wind of this.

They arrived at the tent of the famous Campeador.
As soon as they entered he kissed their hands
and smiled and spoke: "Ah, Don Raquel and Vidas,
I thought you'd forgotten about me!   155
I am exiled from this land, for the king is angry.

So it looks like you'll be getting something of mine.
As long as you live, you won't be the poorer for it!"
Don Raquel and Vidas kiss his hands.
Martín Antolínez concludes the deal: 160
On the security of the chests,
they will give six hundred marks
and guard them well for one year's time.
To this they have pledged their faith and sworn.
If they open the chests beforehand, they are perjured
and the Cid will not give them one penny.   165

Martín Antolínez said, "Let's load the chests in secret.
Take them, Raquel and Vidas, and keep them safe.
I'll go with you and come back with the marks
for the Cid must leave before the rooster crows."

Look at their joy when the chests are loaded!   170
Though the men are strong, they can hardly lift them.
Raquel and Vidas are thrilled with this treasure—
for the rest of their lives, they have it made!

10. The Payment

Raquel came forward to kiss the Cid's hand.
"Campeador, in a good hour you girded on your sword!   175
You are leaving Castile now for foreign parts.
With your luck, you are sure to make great profits.
A fine Moorish coat of crimson leather, My Cid—
I kiss your hand that I may have this gift."

"My pleasure," said the Cid. "Let it be so.
I'll bring one back—if not, deduct it from the chests." 180

[A brief gap in the manuscript. Menéndez Pidal's reconstruction from other sources:

Raquel and Vidas took the chests.
With Martín Antolínez, in secret
they went back to Burgos.]

They spread out a rug in the middle of the room
and upon it a white linen sheet.
First they flung three hundred marks of silver on it.
Don Martín took note without weighing them. 185
The other three hundred they paid him in gold.
His five squires were all heavy laden.

When this was done, hear what he said:
"Well, Don Raquel and Vidas, in your hands I leave the chests.
I, who got them for you, deserve a gift of stockings." 190

11. Something on the Side

Raquel and Vidas stepped aside.
"Let's give him a good gift, since he brought us this business."

"Martín Antolínez, worthy citizen of Burgos,
you have earned a fine gift, and we intend to give it.
For stockings, rich furs, and a good stout coat 195

we will give you thirty marks."
You have earned it, and it's only right
since you bear witness to what we have agreed."

Don Martín thanked them and took the marks.　　　　　　
Eager to leave, he bade goodbye to both.　　　　　　200
Riding out of Burgos, crossing the Arlanzón
he came to the tent of the Campeador.
The Cid received him with open arms:

"Come, Martín Antolínez, my faithful vassal.
The day is coming when you'll get something from me!"　　205

"I come, Campeador, having concluded this business prudently
with six hundred marks for you, and for my share thirty.
Order them to strike the tents. Let's leave in secret
and be in San Pedro de Cardeña when the rooster crows.
There we shall see your wife, that wise and noble lady.　　210
After we rest for a bit, we'll leave the kingdom
as we must, for the date draws near."

12. The Cid prays to Santa María

These words spoken, the camp is struck.
My Cid and his company mount at once.
He turns his horse toward Santa María,　　215
raises his right hand and crosses himself.

"To you I give thanks, oh God who guards heaven and earth.

May your grace be with me, glorious Santa María.
I am about to quit Castile, for the king is angry with me.
I don't know if I will return in all my days.   220
May your power protect me, Gloriosa, in my exile,
help and sustain me both day and night.
If you grant this, and my fortune holds
I will endow you with rich gifts
and pledge to have a thousand masses sung."   225

13. Martín Antolínez visits home

The good man said goodbye with heart and will.
They released the reins and spurred their horses.
Martín Antolínez said, "I will go see the wife who is my solace
and leave her instructions on what to do.
If the king wants to take my possessions, I don't care.   230
I'll be with you before the sun begins to shine."
Martín Antolínez turned toward Burgos.
My Cid spurred onward as fast as he could
with his knights to San Pedro de Cardeña.

14. At the monastery

The cock would soon crow and the dawn begin to break   235
when the Campeador reached San Pedro.
The abbot Don Sancho, a Christian of the Creator
was saying matins as the sun came up.
Doña Ximena was there, with five noble ladies
praying to San Pedro and to God: 240
"You who guide all creatures, protect My Cid the Campeador!"

15. The Cid speaks with the Abbot

The Cid knocked at the door. When they heard who was calling,
God, how great was Don Sancho's joy!
With lamps and candles they rushed to the courtyard
to joyfully welcome the Campeador. Don Sancho said,   245
"I thank God to see you, my good Cid.
Please accept my hospitality."

"Thanks, good abbot, I am greatly in your debt.
I will take supplies for myself and my men.
Because I am going into exile, I will give you fifty marks.   250
If one day I should return, you'll see that doubled.
I don't want to do the monastery
a penny's worth of harm.

For Doña Ximena I give you a hundred marks
to take care of her and her ladies for the year.
Two young daughters I leave behind. Hold them in your arms. 255
I commend them to you, Don Sancho,
take care of them and my wife.
If that's not enough, if you lack for anything,
supply their need and I promise you
for every mark you spend, I'll give you four."   260

The abbot gladly grants his wish.
Now comes Doña Ximena with her children.
Noble ladies hold them in their arms.
Doña Ximena gets down on her knees before the Cid,
weeping and kissing his hands.   265
"Help me, Campeador, born in a fortunate hour!
Because of evil slander you are driven from this land."

16. Farewell to Doña Ximena

"Help me, oh Cid, you of the beautiful beard!
Here you have me and your daughters,
children of tender years,
along with these ladies who serve me.   270
I can see you are about to leave, and we
must part from one another in this life.
Give us counsel, for the love of Santa María!"

He of the beautiful beard stretched out his hands
and embraced his little daughters.   275
He took them to his heart, for he loved them dearly.
From his eyes fell tears, he gave a heavy sigh.

"Ah, Doña Ximena, my dear wife,
I love you like my very soul.
You see we must part in this life.   280
I must go and you must stay behind.
If it please God and Santa María
I may yet give these daughters in marriage.
And if, with luck, I have a few days left,
I will spend them, honored lady, serving you."

17. Knights respond to the call

They prepare a great banquet for the Cid   285
and the bells ring out at San Pedro.

Through all Castile the news is cried:
My Cid the Campeador will leave this land.
To join him some leave houses, others honors.

That day at the bridge of Arlanzón   290
a hundred and fifteen knights have gathered,
all asking about the Campeador.
Martín Antolínez joins up with them
and they head for San Pedro to meet the Cid.

18. THE CID INSTRUCTS HIS TROOPS

When My Cid of Vivar found out   295
that his company was growing stronger
he quickly rode out to greet them.
He smiled when he saw them.
They gathered to kiss his hand.

My Cid spoke from his heart:
"I pray to God the heavenly Father   300
I can do you some good before I die.
Your homes and estates you have left for me—
for all you lose now, I will pay you back double."
My Cid was happy that his force had grown
and so were all the others with him.   305
Six days of the king's term had passed.
Three days remained, no more.
The king ordered watch kept on the Cid
to arrest him if he stayed within these lands—
neither gold nor silver would help him escape.   310

The day was gone and the night was coming on.
He called all his horsemen together:
"Listen, men. Don't be discouraged.
I have little money, but you shall have your part.
Here, then, is what we must do. 315
In the morning, when the cock begins to crow
saddle your horses without delay. In San Pedro
the good abbot will ring the bell for matins
and say the Mass of the Holy Trinity.
When the Mass is over, be ready to ride— 320
the time is near, and we have far to go."

(The prayer of Ximena)

Everyone followed the Cid's command.
Night passed and the morning came.
They saddled their horses when the cocks crowed,
and promptly the matins were rung. 325
As my Cid and his wife went into the church
Doña Ximena threw herself upon the altar steps
and begged the Creator as best she could
to keep the Cid from harm:

"Oh glorious Lord, our Father in heaven 330
you made the sky and earth and sea,
the stars, the moon, and the sun to keep us warm.
You, incarnate in Your mother Mary,
were born, according to Your will, in Bethlehem.
The shepherds praised and glorified You. 335

Three kings of Arabia came to adore You,
Melchoir and Gaspar and Balthazar
with gold and myrrh and frankincense.

"You saved Jonah when he fell into the sea.
You saved Daniel in the evil den of lions. 340
You saved Saint Sebastian in Rome
and Saint Susannah from her false accuser.
"Lord, for thirty years You walked this earth
performing miracles that we must speak of:
You made wine from water, bread from stone, 345
brought Lazarus back from the dead.

"You let the Jews arrest you. Upon Mount Calvary
in a place called Golgatha they put You on the cross
between two thieves, one on either side.
One is now in paradise, but not the other. 350

"Upon the cross You showed Your great power:
Longinus, who was blind from birth
pierced Your side with a spear, and blood came out,
ran down the shaft and stained his hands.

"He raised his hands and touched his face, 355
opened his eyes and looked around.
In that hour he believed in You
and was saved from harm.

"You rose up from the tomb,
broke open the gates of Hell
and brought forth the holy fathers. 360

"You are the King of Kings and Father of All.
I adore and believe in You with all my heart
and beg Saint Peter to help me pray
for my Campeador, that God may keep
him safe when we must part today
and, in this life, bring us back together." 365

(FAREWELLS)

When her prayer was done and Mass was said
they left the church and prepared to part.
The Cid embraced Doña Ximena.
She kissed his hand, weeping, beside herself with grief. 370

He turned to look at the children:
"My daughters, I commend you to our Heavenly Father
We part for now. God only knows when we shall be together."

With weeping like you've never seen
they separated from each other
like a fingernail ripped from the flesh. 375

(DEPARTURE)

My Cid and his vassals are ready to ride.
As he waits, he keeps turning his head and looking back.
Minaya Alvar Fáñez spoke up wisely:
"My Cid, where is your strength?
We must be on our way, not wasting time. 380

All these sorrows will someday turn to joy.
The God who gave us souls will give us counsel."

The abbot Don Sancho was once again advised
to take care of Doña Ximena and her children
and all the ladies with her. Don Sancho knew   385
that he would be well rewarded.

The abbot turned to go, and Minaya told him:
"Abbot, if people come who want to join us,
tell them to follow our tracks.
In towns or in the wastelands they will find us."   390

They release the reins and ride away—
the day draws near when they must leave this land.
My Cid makes camp at Spinaz de Can,
men coming to him that night from all directions.   395
Next morning they mount and ride again.

The loyal Campeador leaves his own land.
On the left they see Sant Estevan, that good city.
To the right, the towers of Alilon, held by the Moors.
They pass by Alcobiella, the last outpost of Castile.
Crossing the road called Quinea,   400
they ford the Duero at Navas de Palos.
My Cid stops to rest at Figueruela
with men still joining him from everywhere.

19. The Dream of the Cid

After dinner My Cid lay down
and slept so well a sweet dream took him.　　　　405
The angel Gabriel came to him and said:

"Ride on, Cid, good Campeador!
No man ever set out at a better time.
As long as you live, you will find success."

When the Cid woke up he crossed himsel　　　　410
and commended himself to God,
greatly delighted with his dream.

20. The Truce Runs Out

The next morning they mounted and rode.
This was the last day of the truce—there were no more.
They came to a halt at the mountains of Miedes.　　　　415

21.

It was still daylight, the sun had not yet set
when the Cid reviewed his troops.
Not counting foot soldiers—all valient men—
he had three hundred lances, all with pennons.

22.

"Feed your horses early, may God save you! 420
If you want to eat, eat. If not, let's ride.
We will cross these mountains, high and wild
and leave King Alfonso's land tonight.
After that, whoever looks for us can find us."

They crossed the sierra by night. When morning came 425
they were already on the downhill slope.
In the midst of a forest wondrous and vast
My Cid called a halt and fed the horses.

He told his men he wished to ride all night.
His good vassals with a whole heart 430
will do what their lord commands.
Before dark they mounted again—
My Cid wanted no one to see them—
and travelled all night without resting.

At a place called Castejón, on the river Henares 435
My Cid and his men set an ambush.
The rest of the night they lay in wait.
Minaya Alvar Fáñez gave his advice:

23. Attack on Castejón

"Now Cid, in a fortunate hour you strapped on your sword!
With a hundred of our company, 440
once we take Castejón by surprise,

[gap in the manuscript, filled by Menéndez Pidal from other sources:

you remain there as our rearguard.
Give me two hundred men to go raiding—
with God's help and your luck we'll bring a fortune back."
"Well spoken, Minaya," said the Cid.]

"You go ahead, then, with two hundred men.
Be sure to take Alvar Alvarez and Alvar Salvadórez
and Galín García, a hardy lance—
good horsemen to help you, Minaya.

"Ride boldly, don't let fear detain you,   445
down the Hita, through Guadalajara.
The advance guard should go as far as Alcalá
and take all the treasure you can.
Leave nothing behind from fear of the Moors.

"I will remain in the rear with a hundred men
and take possession of Castejón, a strong position.   450
If your vanguard runs into trouble
send word back quickly to me
and all Spain shall speak of the help I bring!"
They name those who will go in the vanguard
and those who will stay behind with the Cid.   455
Now dawn has broken and the morning comes.
God, how lovely the sun comes out!

Everyone in Castejón arises.
They open the gates and go outside
to see to their farms and their work.   460
They leave, and they leave the gates open.
Few remain behind in Castejón,
the rest are scattered everywhere.

The Cid springs forth from his ambush
and charges upon Castejón,   465
capturing Moors and Mooresses
and all the livestock wandering about.
Rodrigo rushes the city's gate—
the guards, when they see his attack
are filled with fear and leave it undefended.   470
My Cid Ruy Díaz gallops through the gate,
naked sword in hand,
pursuing and killing fifteen Moors.

Castejón is won, with its gold and silver.
His horsemen bring in the booty   475
and present it to the Cid
as though all this were nothing.

(MINAYA'S RAID)

Meanwhile, the two hundred knights in the vanguard
were riding relentlessly. Minaya's banner
went all the way to Alcalá.
From there they returned with their spoils

up the Henares and back through Guadalajara. 480
Their haul was huge: flocks of sheep and cattle
and garments and other great riches.
Straight ahead flies the flag of Minaya
and no one dares to attack his train.

The raiders return with all their goods
to the Campeador in Castejón. 485
Leaving the castle defended, the Cid rides out
to welcome his company.
He receives Minaya with open arms:

"You have come, Alvar Fáñez, a hardy lance!
Whenever I see you, I expect the best. 490
From all of our booty heaped together
I will give you a fifth if you wish, Minaya."

24. Minaya's oath

"I am grateful, great Campeador
for this fifth you wish to give me.
Alfonso of Castile would be glad to see it. 495
But I give it up and give it back to you.
"I swear to God who dwells on high—
until I satisfy myself, on my good horse
fighting Moors in the field,
plying my lance, setting hand to my sword 500
and dripping blood up to my elbows
in the sight of Ruy Díaz the famous warrior,

I will not take from you a single penny.
Until I have won you something worthwhile
I leave everything in your hands." 505

25. Dividing the Spoils

Their gains were collected together.
The Cid, born in a fortunate hour, considered
that King Alfonso and his troops might come
intending harm to him and his company.
He ordered the goods divided 510
with each man's share being written down.
His nobles received a windfall:
to every one a hundred silver marks
and to each of the foot soldiers fifty.
One fifth remained with the Cid. 515

He could not sell it on the spot
nor give it as a gift. Nor did he wish
to carry the captives in his train.
He spoke with those of Castejón
and sent word to Hita and Guadalajara
to see what they'd pay for his fifth.
Whatever they said, it would be a handsome sum. 520
The Moors figured three thousand silver marks.
Rodrigo was pleased with this amount,
which they paid on the third day without fail.

The Cid did not reckon it wise to occupy

the castle in Castejón. He could have held it, 525
but it was too small, with no source of water.

"These Moors have a peace treaty with Alfonso.
He would attack us here with his entire army.
I need to quit Castejón. Listen, my troops and Minaya!

26. Disposition of Castejón

"What I'm about to say, don't take it badly. 530
We cannot stay in Castejón. King Alfonso
is close by, and he will come after us.
I will not raze the castle. Rather, I set free
a hundred Moors and their Moorish ladies,
that none may speak ill of me. 535
You've all been paid, and no one has been denied.
So tomorrow morning let us mount and ride.
I don't want to fight with my lord Alfonso."

Everyone's happy with what the Cid says.
They go away rich from the castle they've taken, 540
the Moors and their ladies blessing them.

They go up the Henares as far as they can,
through the Alcarrias and straight ahead,
passing the caves of Anquita.
Then over the water, onto the plain of Taranz 545
and down from there as far as they could go.
Between Fáriza and Cetina My Cid sought shelter,

taking great booty wherever he went.
The Moors cannot guess what he has in mind.

Next day My Cid of Vivar broke camp 550
and passing Alhama went down the Hoz
beyond Bobierca and Ateca.
He came to rest above Alcocer
upon a round hill, high and strong.
The river Jalón ran by the town— 555
there was no way to cut off their water.
My Cid Don Rodrigo decided to take Alcocer.

27. The seige of Alcocer

He manned the slopes well,
took firm possession of his positions—
some by the mountain, some by the water. 560
Around the hill, close to the river
My Cid had his men dig a trench
to protect against sudden attack by night or day,
and to let them know that the Cid was here to stay.

28.

Through all that country the news went out
that the Cid had occupied this place, 565
exiled from Christians and come among the Moors.
No one dared to farm the land close by;

My Cid and his vassals kept close watch.
Alcocer's castle began to send them tribute.   570

29.

Payments also came from Teca and Terrer.
The people of Catalayud were filled with foreboding.
My Cid kept up his seige for fifteen weeks.
When he saw that Alcocer would not surrender
he devised a strategem without delay.   575

(The Battle of Alcocer)

He left one tent standing and took the rest,
riding down the Jalón with his banner raised,
his men in their armor with swords strapped on—
a smart move to draw out the enemy.

When the men of Alcocer saw this,
God, how they flattered themselves!   580
"The Cid is out of bread and fodder.
He is fleeing as though from a rout—
in his hurry he even left one tent standing!
Let's sally out and attack him.
We'll win a great treasure
before the men of Terrer can take it—
if they do, you know they'll give us nothing.   585

The tribute we've paid will come back doubled!"

They poured out of Alcocer in a hurry.
The Cid saw them, and rode off in a rout
down the Jalón, with all his men around him.
The men of Alcocer shout "There goes our treasure!" 590
Big and little, all rush out.
Eager to grab him, thinking of nothing else,
they leave their gates wide open, without guard.
The good Campeador now turns his head
and seeing a wide open space
between the castle and the crowd, 595
orders his standard turned around, and spurs his horse.
"Strike them, caballeros, without fear!
With God's grace, the victory is ours!"

They turn about, in the middle of the plain.
God, what great joy they had that morning! 600
My Cid and Alvar Fáñez now spur forward.
Both on good horses that go where they wish,
they cut off the Moors from their castle.

The Cid's vassals struck without mercy.
In about an hour they killed three hundred Moors. 605
Loud cries still coming from the ambush,
those in front now turned toward the castle
and stopped at the gate with drawn swords.
The rest came up when the battle was done.
By this stratagem the Cid had won Alcocer. 610

30. Clemency toward the Moors

Pedro Vermúdez came up with the banner in his hand
and planted it on the highest point.
My Cid Ruy Díaz, born in a fortunate hour, spoke:
"Thanks be to God in heaven and all His saints!
Now we have a better place for horses and their masters."   615

31.

"Listen, Alvar Fáñez and all my men.
In this castle we have won great wealth.
The Moors lie dead; I see few still alive.
We cannot sell these Moors and Mooresses,
and beheading them does us no good.   620
Let us take them back in,
now that we are masters of this place.
We'll live in their houses, and they shall serve us."

32. The Moors ask Valencia for help

My Cid, now in Alcocer with the treasure,
sends for the tent they left behind.

Teca is sad, Terrer is not happy   625
and Catalayud in plunged in gloom.

They send word to the king of Valencia:

"One they call My Cid, Ruy Díaz of Vivar,
being banished by King Alfonso
encamped by Alcocer in a strong position, 630
drew them into an ambush and took the castle.
If you don't advise and aid us, you will lose
Teca, Terrer, and Catalayud, without a doubt.
All will be lost on the river Jalón
as well as Jiloca on the other side." 635

King Tamín heard this with a heavy heart.
"I see three Moorish kings beside me.
Two of you without delay go out.
Take three thousand Moorish soldiers;
those on the frontier will help you too. 640
Take him alive and bring him back to me,
to tell me by what right he invades my country."

Three thousand Moors now mount and ride,
camping that night at Segorbe. 645
The next day they ride and reach Celfa.
They send word all along the frontier—
from all sides men hurry to join them.
Departing from Celfa, also called The Canal,
they ride all day long without resting, 650
camping that night at Catalayud.
Throughout these lands the heralds ride.
In great numbers men gather
to join the two kings, Fáriz and Galve,

and encircle My Cid at Alcocer.   655

33. The Cid besieged

They pitched their tents and took their positions,
their forces increased with huge numbers of men.
Day and night they send out armed patrols.
So many are the scouts, so large the army,   660
they cut off the Cid from the water.
The Cid's men want to go forth to battle—
Rodrigo firmly forbids it.
For three weeks the Moors have them surrounded.

34.

Three weeks past and a fourth begun,   665
My Cid takes council with his troops:
"They have cut off our water, our bread will soon run out.
They won't allow us to escape by night
and their force is a big one for ours to fight.
Tell me, men, what you want to do.   670
Minaya spoke up first, a worthy knight:
"We've been exiled from fair Castile—
if we don't fight the Moors,
they won't give us their bread.
We have a good six hundred knights.
There's only one thing left for us to do—
by God, let's attack them tomorrow!"   675

"That's what I like to hear!" said Rodrigo.
Your words do you honor, Minaya,
and so, I know, will your deeds."

They made all the Moors and Mooresses leave town
so none could see their secret preparations.   680
All day and all night they made ready.

(THE ATTACK ON FÁRIZ AND GALVE)

Next morning as the sun was rising
My Cid and all his men were armed.
He spoke to the troops, as you shall hear:
"Let us all go out. Let none remain behind   685
except for two soldiers to guard the gate.
If we die in the field, they will take the castle.
But if we win, we'll be richer than ever!

"You, Pedro Vermúdez, take my standard,
good man that you are, and bear it faithfully.   690
But don't go forward until I tell you to!"
Pedro kissed the Cid's hand and took up the banner.

They opened the gates and galloped out.
The Moorish scouts saw them and ran back to camp.
How the Moors hurried to arm themselves!   695
The earth quaked with the thunder of drums

as the Moors armed and rushed into ranks.

On the Moorish side were two great banners,
two ranks of mixed soldiers—who could number them?
The ranks of the Moors now began to move forward   700
to meet the Cid's men hand to hand.

"Stay put, men, right where you are.
No one moves until I give the order!"

Pedro Vermúdez can't stand the suspense.
Banner in hand, he sets spur to his horse.   705
"God be with you, good Campeador!
I'm going to plant your standard
in the main ranks of the Moors.
All those who owe you loyalty,
let's see how they defend it!"

The Cid says "For God's sake, no!"

Pedro says "Nothing can stop me now!"   710
He spurs forward, setting the standard of the Cid
in the Moors' main battle line.
The Moors rush to win the standard
raining great blows upon Pedro
but they cannot break his armor.

The Cid shouts
"Help him, for goodness sake!"

35.

The men hold their shields to their hearts   715
lower their lances with their pennons
lean forward over their saddles
and launch their charge courageously.

"Attack them, knights, for the love of God!   720
I am Ruy Díaz the Cid, the Campeador of Vivar!"

Everyone rushes at the rank where Pedro Vermúdez stands.
Three hundred lances, each with its pennon
kill three hundred Moors with as many blows.
They turn and charge and kill three hundred more.   725

36.

See so many lances rise and fall
so many shields shattered and pierced
so many coats of armor stained and broken
so many white pennons pulled out, red with blood
so many good horses running riderless.   730
The Moors all shout "Mohammad!"
and the Christians "Santiago!"
Before long a thousand and three hundred Moors are dead.

37.

How well they fought in their gilded saddles:
My Cid Ruy Díaz, the great warrior
Minaya Albar Fáñez, who ruled Zorita   735
Martín Antolínez, the good man of Burgos
Muño Gustioz, Rodrigo's household knight
Martín Muñoz, commander of Monte Mayor
Alvar Alvarez and Alvar Salvadórez
Galín García, the good knight of Aragón   740
and Féliz Muñoz, the nephew of the Cid!
These and the rest all rallied to the banner
and to My Cid the Campeador.

38. MINAYA IN TROUBLE. THE CID AGAINST FÁRIZ.

The Moors killed the horse of Minaya Albar Fáñez.
The Christian troops rushed to his rescue.   745
His lance now broken, he grabbed his sword
and, though on foot, still dealt out heavy blows.

My Cid Ruy Díaz saw his need
and attacked a well-mounted Moorish aguazil.
He gave such a swing with his good right arm   750
that the Moor, cut in half at the waist,
fell dead to the ground.

He brought the Moor's horse to Minaya Alvar Fáñez.

"Mount up, Minaya—you are my good right arm!
Today I will surely need your help. The Moors
stand firm and have not fled the field." 755

Minaya mounted the horse and, sword in hand
fought his way bravely through the Moorish troops
freeing the souls of those he overtook.

My Cid Ruy Díaz, born in a fortunate hour
took three cuts at the Moorish King Fáriz. 760
The first two failed, the third struck home—
blood spurted and ran down his coat of mail.
Fáriz pulled his reins and fled from the field—
by that blow the battle was won.

39. ROUT AND PURSUIT

Martín Antolínez also struck King Galvez, 765
shattered the rubies adorning his crest,
cut through his helmet and into the flesh.
You know Galve decided not to wait
for another blow.

Kings Fáriz and Galve were defeated—
what a great day for Christendom 770
with Moors fleeing in every direction!
The Cid's men striking all they overtook,
King Fáriz took shelter in Terrer.
They didn't take King Galve—

he rode for Catalayud as hard as he could. 775
The Cid's pursuit ended there.

40. Minaya fulfills his pledge. The Cid returns.

His horse running hard, Minaya Alvar Fáñez
killed thirty-four of those Moors.
His sword bit deep, blood stained his arm 780
and went running down to his elbow.
Minaya said, "Now I am satisfied.
The good news will fly to Castile
that My Cid has been victorious in battle."

Struck down relentlessly in the pursuit,
so many Moors lay dead that few remained. 785
The Cid's men return with Rodrigo
riding his fine horse, hood pulled back—
my God, what a beautiful beard!
Chain mail on his shoulders, sword in hand 790
he watched his troops come in, and said:
"Thanks be to God who dwells on high
that we have the victory in such a battle!"

(The spoils of battle)

The Cid's men plundered the Moorish camp
of shields and arms and other rich possessions. 795

When they brought it all in
they had five hundred and ten Moorish horses.
There was great joy among the Christian troops:
they had lost fewer than fifteen in battle.
They carry more gold and silver than they can count.
All the Christians are made rich men.   800

They now let the Moors come back to the castle.
The Cid insists even they should have a share—
it gives Rodrigo and his men great joy
to hand out so much wealth and treasure.
The Cid's fifth included a hundred horses,   8055
and God, how well he paid his vassals,
foot soldiers and horsemen alike!
Born in a fortunate hour, the Cid
divides things up so that all are satisfied.

(A MISSION TO CASTILE)

"Hear me, Minaya—you are my own right arm!   810
From this wealth the Creator has granted us
take what you wish with your own hand.

"I want to send you to Castile
with news of this battle we have won.
To King Alfonso, who is angry with me   815
I wish to send a gift of thirty horses,
all fully furnished with saddles and gear,
and a sword hung from every saddle."

Minaya said, "I will do this gladly."

41.

"Here is gold and silver—a bootful, brimming over. 820
Pay for a thousand masses at Santa María of Burgos
and give the rest to my wife and daughters
that they may pray for me day and night.
They will be rich women if I survive." 825

42.

Minaya Alvar Fáñez is pleased with this.
Men are chosen to go with him.
They feed the horses. Night has come.
My Cid calls a meeting with his men:

43.

"You return, Minaya, to fair Castile.
To our friends you can certainly say 830
'God helped us, and we won the battle.'
When you come back, you may find us here.
If not, follow when you find out where we are.
Lances and swords must be our shelter now—
there's no other way to survive in this barren land." 835

44. The Moors make a deal

Everything ready, Minaya left next morning.
The Cid and his army stayed behind.
The land was poor and wretched.
Every day they kept watch on the Cid,
the Moors of the frontier and foreign parts.   840
They take counsel with King Fáriz, who has healed.

The people of Teca and Terrer
and Catalayud, a more notable town
have struck a bargain, written down the deal:
they buy Alcocer for three thousand silver marks.   845

45.

My Cid Ruy Díaz has sold Alcocer,
and how well he paid his own vassals!
Peons and caballeros, everyone is rich,
not a poor man left among them.
He who serves a good lord lives in joy.   850

46. The Cid abandons Alcocer

When the Cid made ready to leave the castle
the Moors and their ladies began to lament:
"You are leaving, My Cid? Our prayers go with you.
We are content, lord, with what you have done for us."

When My Cid left Alcocer					855
the Moors and their ladies all began to weep.
Raising his standard, the Cid rode forth.
Along the Jalón he spurred straight ahead.
Birds of good omen were seen when they left the river.

The people of Terrer were pleased
and even more Catalayud,					860
but those of Alcocer grieved his going—
he had done them a great deal of good.
Ruy Díaz the Campeador spurred onward,
camping at last on a rocky outcrop
high above Mont Real.
Its cliffs are towering and grand
and fear no attack from any quarter.			865

He first made Daroca pay tribute
then Molina on the other side
and thirdly Teruel, which stood in front.
He also had Celfa del Canal in hand.

47. Minaya's Meeting with Alfonso

May God grant grace to My Cid Ruy Díaz!			870
Minaya Alvar Fáñez has gone to Castile
and presented thirty horses to the king.
When he saw them he smiled with pleasure.
"God bless you, Minaya, who gave you these?"

"My Cid Ruy Díaz, who strapped on his sword
in a fortunate hour. 875
He conquered two Moorish kings in that battle
and the booty, my lord, was enormous.
To you, honored king, he sends this present.
He kisses your hands and feet
and begs for mercy, should God grant it." 880

The king said, "It's still too early
for an exile who lost his lord's favor
to be welcomed back after just three weeks.
But since it was won from the Moors, I accept this gift
and even take pleasure in the Cid's success. 885

Regarding what I took from you, Minaya,
your lands and honors shall be restored.
Come and go as you please—
from now on you are in my favor.
As for the Campeador, I am saying nothing.

48.

"Furthermore, Minaya, I will tell you 890
that those of my reign who wish to go,
brave and valiant, to help the Cid
may have my permission and keep their property."

Minaya Alvar Fáñez kissed his hands.

"Thank you, my natural lord and king 895
for this favor now, and those to come."

49. Minaya's return

"Go freely through Castile, Minaya
and return to the Cid without delay."

Now I want to tell you about the Cid.
He camped at El Poyo, on a rocky mount. 900
Among Christians and Moors, that place on the map
would be known as "The Chair of the Cid."
There he raided the countryside
and laid the river Monzón under tribute.
News of the Cid reached Zaragossa. 905
The Moors are not pleased; it weighs heavy on them.

A full fifteen weeks the Cid stayed there.
When he saw that Minaya would be delayed
he marched away overnight with all his men,
leaving El Poyo behind. 910

Beyond Teruel Rodrigo passed
and pitched camp in the pine grove of Tévar.
He plundered all the lands around,
exacting tribute as far as Zaragossa.

Three weeks after this was done 915
Minaya came back from Castile.

Two hundred knights were with him, bearing swords,
not counting, of course, the foot soldiers.

When My Cid saw Minaya appear
he galloped out to embrace him, 920
kissing his mouth and his eyes.
Minaya told him everything, without exception.
The Cid smiled a beautiful smile:
"Thanks be to God and His holy power—
as long as you live, things go well for me, Minaya!" 925

50.

God, how the whole army rejoiced at Minaya's arrival,
bringing greetings from cousins and brothers
and friends they had left behind!

51.

God, how he of the beautiful beard was glad 930
that Minaya paid for a thousand masses
and gave his greetings to his wife and daughters!
God, how the Cid was overjoyed!
"Long life to you, Alvar Fáñez!"

52. RAIDING AND RICH BOOTY

The Campeador did not delay   935
in raiding the lands all around him.
On the third day he returned
leaving the lands of Alcañiz scorched and black.

53.

News of the raid spreads far and wide,
frightening Monzón and Huesa.   940
Zaragoza, which pays tribute, is content,
fearing no outrage from the Cid

54.

They come back to camp with their booty,
everyone pleased, for the plunder is great.
The Cid is glad, and Minaya even more so.   945
The great man couldn't help but smile:

"Caballeros, I'm telling you the truth—
he who stays in one place loses out!
Tomorrow morning we will ride.
Let's pull up stakes and move on."   950

The Cid moved to the pass of Alucant.
From there he made a ten-day run
as far as Huesa and Mont Albán.
Word spread everywhere of the damage
the exile from Castile had done.   955

55. The Count of Barcelona swears revenge

News came to the Count of Barcelona
that the Cid had overrun his land.
Greatly aggrieved, he took this as an insult.

56.

The Count, a great braggart, spoke foolishly: 960
"My Cid of Vivar has done me great wrong.
In my own court he insulted me—
struck my nephew and never made amends.
Now he is raiding land under my protection.
I never challenged him nor turned against him, 965
but now that he has sought me out
I shall demand satisfaction."

Quickly he gathered great forces—
Moors and Christians came to him—
and marched straight for My Cid of Vivar.
Three days and two nights they traveled 970
and found him in the pine woods of Tévar.
With such forces, the Count
was confident of taking him in hand.

My Cid, lugging a lot of booty
came down the mountain and into a valley.
Count Ramón's message had arrived. 975

The Cid, when he heard it, replied:
"Tell the Count not to take it so hard.
I have nothing of his, so let me go in peace."

The Count replied, "Not so fast!
He will pay me for past and present injuries.　　　　980
This exile will soon find out
what kind of man he comes to dishonor!"

The messenger returned as fast as he could.
The Cid now realized
he wouldn't get out of this without a fight.

57. THE CID PREPARES HIS MEN FOR BATTLE

"Now my knights, put aside your plunder—　　　　985
quickly get ready and take up arms.
Count Ramón comes to engage us in battle.
He has a great host of Moors and Christians
and won't let us leave without fighting.

"They're coming for us, so the battle will be here.　　　　990
Cinch up your saddles and throw on your armor.
They'll be riding downhill, wearing slippers.
Their cinches will be slack, their saddles small.
We'll be on good Galician saddles, wearing riding boots—
with a hundred horsemen we'll defeat them all　　　　995.

"Before they reach the plain, we'll show our lances.
For each one you hit, you'll see three empty saddles.
Count Ramón Berenguer will see, in this pine wood of Tévar
what kind of man he's come to plunder!"

58

By the time the Cid finished his speech   1000
his men were all ready, armed and mounted.
They could see the Catalans coming down the hill.
At the foot of the slope, where the plain began,
the Cid ordered his men to attack.
They did so gladly and with a will,   1005
using their lances and pennons so well
they wounded many, and unhorsed the others.
The Cid, born in a fortunate hour, won the battle
and took the good Count Ramón prisoner.

59. COUNT RAMÓN LOSES HIS APPETITE

The Cid had won the sword Colada,
worth more than a thousand silver marks.   1010
This victory brought honor to his beard.
He brought the Count as prisoner to his tent
and ordered his faithful vassals to stand guard.

Leaving the tent, he jumped for joy
as his men came crowding all around him.   1015

The Cid was pleased with their enormous plunder.

They prepared a great feast for My Cid,
but Count Ramón had little appetite.
They brought food and set it before him.
He refused to eat, rejecting it with scorn: 1020

"I won't eat a mouthful for all of Spain.
Better abandon my body and give up the ghost
since I've been beaten by such ill-shod outcasts!"

60.

Listen to what My Cid said:
"Count, eat this bread and drink this wine.   1025
Do as I say and you shall go free. If not,
for as long as you live you will never see Christendom."

61.

Count Ramón replied:
"You eat, Don Rodrigo, and enjoy yourself,
but I intend to die, and will not eat."

For three days they could not agree.   1030
While the Cid's men divided the spoils of battle
he would not eat a morsel of bread.

62.

My Cid said, "Count, eat something—
if you don't, you'll never see your Christian country.
If you will just eat, to please me
I will set you and two of your nobles free." 1035

When he heard this, the Count cheered up.
"If you do what you promise, Cid
as long as I live I will be amazed."

"Then eat up, Count, and when you're full
you and two others will be released. 1040

"What you lost and I won on the field,
you know you're not getting one bad penny back.
I need it and so do my vassals
who share this beggar's life with me.
Taking from you and others, we meet our needs. 1045
This is my life for as long as our Father pleases,
to suffer the anger of the king in exile."

The Count was content, and asked for water
to wash his hands. They brought it at once. 1050
With two other nobles the Cid granted him,
the Count pitched in—God, he ate with a will!

The Cid sat beside him and said,
"Count, if you don't eat well and please me

we'll stay right here and never part again." 1055

"Fine with me," he said.
He and his knights attacked the food.
The Cid was greatly amused to watch
the Count's skillful play of hands.

"If you please, My Cid, we are ready to go. 1060
Please call for our horses now, for we must trot.
I've not eaten so well since I became a Count—
the flavor of this meal won't be forgot."
They give them three palfreys with excellent saddles
along with rich fur coats and cloaks. 1065
The man from Castile escorted them from camp.

"Now go, Count, a free man once more!
I'm in your debt for what you've left behind.
If you ever decide you want it back, 1070
you'll find me here. If not, look me up:
You'll either give me more of yours
or take back some of mine."

"Rest easy, My Cid, you're safe from us.
I've paid you enough for one year— 1075
we won't come looking for you again."

63.

The Count spurred forward, eager to get away.

He turned his head and looked behind,
still afraid that the Cid would change his mind.
But never, not for anything in this world   1080
would that great man stoop to treachery.

The Count is gone. My Cid Ruy Díaz of Vivar
calls his troops together to celebrate
the many and wondrous treasures they have won.

Second *Cantar*

64. THE CID REACHES THE SEA

Here we take up the story of the Cid. 1085
His men are so rich they cannot count it all.
He has occupied the pass of Alucat, and left behind
Zaragoza, Huesa, Mont Albán.

Down to the salt sea he fights his way, 1090
toward the rising sun. My Cid
has won Xérica, Onda, Almenar
and conquered the country around Burriana.

65.

Our Father in heaven was helping him.
When he captured Murviedro too, 1095
he knew he was under God's protection.
Inside Valencia, fear began to spread.

66. THE CID ENCIRCLED

The Valencians are filled with dread,
you know they are not pleased.

They hold a council and conclude
they will besiege the Cid.
They march all night. As morning dawns   1100
they are pitching their tents all around Murviedro.

When the Cid saw this, he was filled with wonder.
"I thank You, heavenly Father!
Here we are in their country, doing all kinds of damage
drinking their wine and eating their bread—
they have every right to besiege us.   1105

"This won't be over without a battle.
Send word to those who owe us help—
some to Xérica, others to Alucat,
from there to Onda and on to Almenar,
then let those of Burriana come.   1110
We'll get this battle going
and I trust to God it will turn out well."

By the third day everyone had gathered.
The man born in a fortunate hour addressed them:

"Listen my troops, may God help you!   1115
Ever since we left clean Christendom—
not by choice, but because we had to—
things have gone well for us, thank God.
Now the Valencians have us encircled.
If we want to remain in this country   1120
we must teach them a lesson they won't forget.

67.

"The night has gone and the morning comes.
I want you all ready, horsed and armed,
and then we'll go take a look at that army.
We are exiles in a foreign land— 1125
out there we'll see who earns his keep!"

68. PLAN OF ATTACK

Hear what Minaya Albar Fáñez said:
"Campeador, we will do as you wish.
Give me a hundred knights, I ask no more.
You and the others attack from the front, 1130
hitting them hard and fast.
I and my men will come in from the flank
and I trust God the victory will be ours."
The Cid was pleased with what Minaya said.

That morning, as they armed themselves, 1135
each man knew what he had to do.

The Cid rides out to attack at dawn.
"In the name of God and St. James the Apostle
charge them, caballeros, with all your heart and will—
for I am the Cid, Ruy Díaz of Vivar! 1140

You should have seen the tent cords cut,
stakes pulled up and poles knocked down!

The Moors are many, they're trying to regroup
when Alvar Fáñez attacks from the other side.

Against their will they must give up and flee. 1145
On foot or horseback those escape who can.
Two Moorish kings are killed in the rout—
as far as Valencia they chase them back.

Great were the spoils the Cid had won.
They stripped the camp and headed home:
taking Cebolla and everything before it 1150
they returned in triumph to Murviedro.
There was great rejoicing in the town.

The Cid's fame, you know, is spreading far
even to lands beyond the sea.
Valencia is full of fear.
They don't know where to turn. 1155

69.

The Cid and all his company are joyful
that God has helped them gain the victory.
He sent forth raiders. Riding by night
they went as far as Gujera and Xátiva 1160
and, farther down, the town of Denia.
Down to the sea they pillaged Moorish lands,
capturing Peña Cadiella
and the roads leading in and out.

70.

When the Cid captured Peña Cadiella
it grieved them in Xátiva and Gujera. 1165
In Valencia their sorrow knew no bounds.

71.

Plundering and seizing Moorish land,
sleeping by day and raiding by night,
the Cid spent three years taking towns.

72. DESPERATION IN VALENCIA

He had taught the Valencians a lesson— 1170
they didn't dare go outside to meet him.
Laying waste to their fields and gardens,
year after year the Cid cut off their food.

The Valencians grieved, not knowing what to do.
They couldn't get bread from anywhere. 1175
Father could not help son, nor son his father,
nor could friend comfort friend.
A hard fate surely, sirs, to have no bread,
to see your wives and children die of hunger.

Disaster looked them in the face, and they were helpless. 1180
They sent for the king of Morocco, but he

was at war with the king of the Atlas Mountains
and could send neither help nor relief.

When the Cid heard of this, his heart rejoiced.
He left Murviedro, riding overnight.   1185
Dawn found him in the lands of Mont Real.
He sent heralds to Navarre and Aragón.
Through the lands of Castile he spread the news:
"if anyone wants to trade poverty for riches,
come join the Cid, who plans to ride   1190
to besiege and win Valencia for the Christians.

73.

"Whoever comes with me to Valencia,
let him come freely and of his own will.
I will wait for him three days at Canal de Celfa."

74. THE SIEGE OF VALENCIA

Thus spoke My Cid, who was born in a fortunate hour,   1195
and returned to Murviedro which he had taken.
His heralds went everywhere.
Quickly responding to the smell of treasure,
crowds of good Christians flocked to join him.
My Cid, growing richer by the day   1200
was glad to see them come together.

My Cid Ruy Díaz would not wait any longer.
He threw himself upon Valencia.
Encircling the city completely,
he would not let anyone in or out.   1205

The news went resounding everywhere.
More men are joining the Cid than leaving him.

He gave them a truce to try to get help—
for nine months his siege lay upon them.
Come the tenth, they were forced to surrender.   1210

Great was the joy that day
when My Cid won Valencia
and entered the city at last!
His foot soldiers now were all mounted knights,
and who could count all the gold and silver?
Everyone there that day was rich!   1215

My Cid Don Rodrigo took his fifth—
in money alone it was thirty thousand marks
and as for the goods, who could count them?
The Campeador and all his men rejoiced
to see their flag on the castle's highest tower.   1220

75. THE KING OF SEVILLE ATTACKS

Then My Cid rested, with all his men.

When the king of Seville heard the news
that Valencia was lost, since no one helped it
he set out with thirty thousand troops.

Fighting near the farms and gardens   1225
My Cid of the long beard routed them.
The pursuit went all the way to Xátiva—
you should have seen the confusion
as they crossed the river Xúcar
Moors caught in the current, forced to drink water.

The king of Seville escaped, wounded thrice.   1230
My Cid returned home with all of his plunder.
Great as the gains from Valencia were, this rout
proved even richer—the humblest soldier
gained a hundred marks of silver.
You see how the fame of this knight has grown.   1235

76. A Plan to Keep His Troops

There is joy among the Christians with the Cid.
His beard is growing longer every day.
So my Cid said:
"For the love of King Alfonso, who has banished me,   1240
no shears shall touch it; not one whisker will be cut.
Let the Moors and the Christians talk about it."

My Cid is relaxing in Valencia
with Minaya Alvar Fáñez at his side.
Those who went into exile with Rodrigo

have all been richly rewarded 1245
with houses in the city and estates.
My Cid goes on proving his love.
Those who left Castile with him
and those who joined him later, all are happy.

My Cid can see that now they have such riches
they would gladly take leave if they could. 1250

My Cid gave an order, advised by Minaya,
that none of his men might leave
without kissing his hand. If not,
they would be pursued, arrested,
stripped of their goods, and hung.

All this arranged, he took counsel with Alvar Fáñez: 1255
"If it seems good to you, Minaya, I'd like a list
of everyone here who's won anything with me,
all written down and counted up,
so if any man flees or goes missing 1260
his possessions can be returned to me
by my vassals keeping watch on Valencia."

"A good plan," said Minaya.

77. A Gift for the King

He ordered them all to come to court.
When they'd gathered, he had them counted.
My Cid had three thousand six hundred men. 1265

With joy in his heart, he began to smile.

"Thank God and Santa María, Minaya!
With far fewer men than these we left Vivar.
Now we are rich, and we shall be richer still.

"If it's alright with you, and not too much trouble   1270
I'd like to send you to Castile, Minaya,
where we have inherited lands,
to see King Alfonso, my natural lord.
Out of the gains we have made here
I'd like you to take him a hundred horses.
Please kiss his hands for me
and urgently plead, if it pleases his mercy   1275
that I may bring my wife and daughters here.

"I shall send for them. Remember this message:
The wife and daughters of the Cid
shall be escorted with the greatest honor   1280
to these foreign lands that we have won."

Minaya said "I will do it gladly."

The conversation over, they got ready.
My Cid gave Alvar Fáñez a hundred men
for an escort along the way, and to San Pedro
asked them to take a thousand silver marks   1285
to give to the Abbot, Don Sancho.

78. The Arrival of Don Jerónimo

While they were rejoicing at this news,
out of the east a priest had come—
Bishop Don Jerónimo by name,
learned in letters and very wise,   1290
a tough warrior on horse or on foot.

He came to ask about the Cid's brave deeds,
sighing to see himself in the field
against the Moors, saying that if he ever tired
of fighting with his own two hands
let no Christian ever mourn him.   1295

The Cid was happy to hear of him.
"Listen Minaya: by Him who dwells above,
when God lends a hand we'll accept it gratefully.
I wish to create a bishopric in Valencia
and give it to this good Christian.   1300
Take this news with you to Castile."

79.

Alvar Fáñez liked what the Cid had said.
They appointed Don Jerónimo as Bishop
in Valencia, where he could well become rich.
God, how glad was all of Christendom   1305
to see a Bishop in Valencia!
Joyful, Minaya said goodbye and left.

80.

The lands of Valencia now at peace,
Alvar Fáñez headed for Castile.
I'll spare you his stops; I've no wish to recount them.   1310
There he asked where he might find Alfonso.
The king had gone to San Fagunt
but come back to Carrión, where he might find him.
Minaya was happy to hear this
and headed straight there with his presents.   1315

81.

King Alfonso had just been hearing Mass—
Minaya arrived at an opportune time.
He sank to his knees in front of all the people,
fell at Alfonso's feet in sorrow,
kissed the king's hands, and spoke these fitting words: 1320

82. Minaya Asks a Favor of the King

"Mercy, King Alfonso, for the love of God!
My Cid kisses his lord's hands and feet—
may he have your grace, as God grants you His.
You have exiled him, he is out of favor,   1325
but he still does well in foreign lands:
He has won Xérica and Onda,
taken Almenar, and what's more, Murviedro,

captured Cebolla and Castejón
and a strong fort, Peña Cadiella.   1330
Besides all this, he is lord of Valencia—
with his own hand he appointed a bishop there.

He has fought five battles and won them all—
great are the riches God has given him.
Here is a token that I speak the truth: 1335
a hundred horses, big and fast,
each one equipped with a saddle and harness.
He kisses your hands and begs you to accept them.
He considers himself your vassal, you his lord."

The king raised his right hand and crossed himself.   1340
"May Saint Isidore bless me! My heart is pleased
at the great wealth the Campeador has won—
pleased with the deeds the Cid has done!
I accept these horses he sends as a gift."

But if the king was pleased, García Ordóñez was not.   1345
"It seems in the Moorish lands there are no men
if the Cid can do whatever he pleases there."

The king told the Count, "No more such talk!
In every way, he does more for me than you do."

Now Minaya spoke up manfully: 1350
"The Cid asks for one favor, if it please you—
that his wife Ximena and their two daughters
might leave the monastery where he left them
and go to join him in Valencia."

To this the king replied, "With all my heart. 1355
While they're in my land, they shall have an escort
to keep them from insult and injury and dishonor.
Once they leave my kingdom,
see that you and the Cid take care of them.

"Hear me, my vassals and all my court! 1360
I don't want the Cid to suffer any loss.
All those vassals who call him lord
whose estates I took away, I give them back.
Let them enjoy their lands wherever he goes.
I free their bodies from harm and fault 1365
so that they can serve him."

Minaya Alvar Fáñez kissed his hand.
The king smiled and spoke graciously:
"Those who wish to serve the Campeador
have my leave to go, and may God bless them. 1370
We will gain more by this than by dishonor."

The Infantes of Carrión spoke aside to one another:
"The fame of the Cid has really grown.
To marry his daughters would be to our advantage.
But we dare not suggest such a thing— 1375
My Cid comes from Vivar, and we from the
Counts of Carrión.
They mentioned it to no one; the matter rested there.

Alvar Fáñez bade the king farewell.
"You're leaving, Minaya—go with the Creator's grace!

Take a royal officer along. You'll find him useful.　　　1380
If you escort the ladies, attend to their every wish.
Give them whatever they need, as far as Medinaceli.
Beyond that, the Campeador will take care of them."
Minaya said goodbye and left the court.

83. Minaya escorts the ladies from Castile

The Infantes of Carrión rode out with him.　　　1385
"You're always a great help. Please do this for us:
Give our greetings to My Cid, Rodrigo of Vivar.
Tell him we'll help him any way we can.
He has nothing to lose by being friends with us."

Minaya replied, "I can do this without any trouble."　　　1390

He went on, the Infantes turned back.
He headed for San Pedro and the ladies.
How great was their joy when they saw him appear!
Minaya, dismounting, went into the church to pray.
When finished, he spoke to the ladies:　　　1395

"I bow to you, Doña Ximena. God keep you from harm,
you and both of your daughters!
My Cid sends his greetings from far away.
I left him both well and wealthy.
The king in his grace has released you　　　1400
to go with me to Valencia, which we have won.
If only the Cid can see you safe and well

all will be joy, without a single care."
"May the Creator make it so!" Doña Ximena said.

Minaya Alvar Fáñez chose three knights 1405
and sent them to My Cid in Valencia.
"Say to the Campeador—may God protect him—
the king has released to me his wife and daughters
and ordered an escort through his lands.
In fifteen days, God willing, 1410
I and his wife and daughters will be with him
and all their good ladies, as many as they have."
The knights leave with this in mind.
Minaya Alvar Fáñez stays behind.

You should have seen the caballeros, coming from everywhere 1415
wanting to join My Cid in Valencia.
They begged Alvar Fáñez to help them.
He said "I will do this gladly."
Sixty-five caballeros have come to Minaya
besides the hundred he brought with him, 1420
a good company gathered to escort the ladies.

Minaya gave the Abbot five hundred marks.
I'll tell you what he did with the other five:
he bought for Doña Ximena and her daughters
and the other ladies who served them 1425
the finest clothing he could find in Burgos,
with palfreys and mules to make an impressive show.

The ladies all fitted out,

Minaya was about to mount his horse 1430
when Raquel and Vidas suddenly appeared
and threw themselves at his feet.

"Have mercy, Minaya, noble knight!
The Cid has undone us if he does not help us.
We'll forgive the interest on his loan
provided he returns the capital."

"I'll speak about it with the Cid, God willing. 1435
You will be rewarded for what you've done."

"May the Creator command it!" say Raquel and Vidas.
"If not, we'll set out from Burgos to find him."

Minaya returned to San Pedro, where many
have gathered round him. Ready to ride, 1440
they are sorry to part from the Abbot.

"May the Creator protect you, Alvar Fáñez!
For me, kiss the hand of the Campeador.
Let him not forget this monastery.
All the days of his life he gives us aid, 1445
his honor will increase."

Minaya says, "I will do it with good will."

Now they say goodbye and ride away.
The king's official comes along as escort.
Throughout the king's lands they are well supplied. 1450

In five days they arrive at Medina,
where the ladies will wait with Alvar Fáñez.

(THE CID'S MEN AND ABENGALVÓN GO TO
MEET THEM)

I will tell you about the knights who took the message:
As soon as the Cid heard the news
his heart was pleased and he rejoiced: 1455

"He who sends a good messenger can expect the same.
You, Muño Gustioz and Pedro Vermúdez,
Martín Antolínez, loyal man of Burgos,
and Bishop Don Jerónimo, worthy priest,   1460
ride with a hundred knights arrayed for battle.

"Through Santa María you shall pass
and come to Molina farther on.
It belongs to Abengalvón, my friend in peace.
He'll join you with another hundred knights.   1465
Head for Medina as quick as you can.
They tell me my wife and children
are waiting there with Alvar Fáñez.

"With greatest honor escort them here.
I'll stay in this city which cost me so much to win—   1470
it would be madness to leave it now.
I'll hold Valencia, my inheritance."

This said, they got ready to ride.
They covered ground as quickly as they could,
passing through Santa María, sleeping at Fronchales.   1475
The next day they stopped at Molina.
The Moor Abengalvón, when he heard the news
went forth to greet them with great joy.

"Come, vassals of my natural friend!
You know this is not a burden but a pleasure!"   1480

Muño Gustioz spoke up without delay:
"My Cid greets you and asks you
to join us quickly with a hundred horsemen.
His wife and daughters are in Medina.
He bids you go to them, escort them here,   1485
and not leave their side till they reach Valencia."

"I will gladly do it," said Abengalvón.
That night he gave them a feast
and was ready to go the next morning.
They asked for a hundred knights,
he brought two hundred.   1490

They crossed the mountains wild and high.
Without fear they passed through the thicket of Taranz,
descending into the valley of Arbujuelo.

In Medina a heavy guard was mounted.
Seeing armed troops, Minaya sent two knights
to find out the truth. They went with a will   1495

and without delay. One stayed with the escort,
the other went back to Minaya.

"The Cid's forces have sought us out.
Pedro Vermúdez is here,
and Muño Gustioz, your faithful friends.
Martín Antolínez of Burgos,   1500
Bishop Don Geronimo, the loyal priest
and lord Abangalvon, who brings his men
out of his love for the Cid, to honor him.
They're all coming together, and will soon be here."

"Let's mount up, then," said Minaya.   1505
They did so quickly, without delay.
A hundred rode out, not a bad-looking bunch,
their handsome horses arrayed in silks
with bells on their breastplates.
Shields were slung from the riders' necks,
their hands bore lances with pennons   1510
so that the others would have no doubt
how well Minaya had managed things
when he left Castile with the ladies.

First they met the Cid's scouts,
who put on a show of arms in play—
there was good fun along the Jalón that day.   1515
When the others arrived, they bowed before Alvar Fáñez.
When Abengalvón laid eyes on him
he smiled and embraced Minaya,
kissing him on each shoulder, as was his custom.

"Good day to you, Minaya Alvar Fáñez! 1520
You do us honor by bringing these ladies,
the wife of the Cid and his daughters.
We must do them honor, for such is his fortune
that even if we wished, we could not harm him.
In war or in peace, what's ours is his— 1525
I hold him dull-witted who does not know this truth."

84. THE MOOR'S HOSPITALITY

Minaya Alvar Fáñez smiled. "Abengalvón,
you're a friend of his who never fails!
If God allows this soul to see the Cid again,
you won't be a loser for what you've done here. 1530
But now let's relax, for our dinner is ready."

Abengalvón said "I'm delighted with your hospitality.
Before the third day I'll return it twice over."

They entered Medina. Minaya feasted them
and all were delighted with how they were served. 1535
The king's officer called for the bill—
the Cid would be honored in Valencia
by this grand banquet in Medina.
The king paid for it all, Minaya spent nothing.

Night had passed and morning come. 1540
They heard Mass and then mounted.
Leaving Medina, they forded the Jalón

and quickly spurred along the Arbuxuelo.
Crossing the plain of Taranz
they came to Molina, which Abengalvón commanded. 1545

Bishop Don Jerónimo, that good and faithful Christian
watched over the ladies day and night.
His good warhorse pacing ahead of his armor,
he and Alvar Fáñez rode together.

They enter Molina, a fine and wealthy town. 1550
The Moor Abengalvón is a gracious host.
Whatever they wish is theirs—
he even pays to have their horses shod.
As for Minaya and the ladies,
God, how he honored them!

Next morning they rode. Along the way 1555
the Moor served them well and faithfully,
spending his own money, taking none of theirs.
Amid all this honor and rejoicing
they come within three leagues of Valencia.

85.

To My Cid in Valencia they sent a message. 1560
He was never happier in all his life
than hearing his loved ones were near.
He quickly sent two hundred knights
to receive Minaya and the noble ladies. 1565

He stayed in Valencia to watch and guard it,
knowing Minaya had things well in hand.

86. The Cid's wife and daughters enter Valencia

See how the knights receive Minaya
and the ladies and children and their companions.
My Cid ordered his household troops   1570
to guard well the castle and other high towers
and all the gates, the entrances and exits.

He ordered them to bring him Babieca.
He had won the horse but a short time before
and didn't know how it would run
or respond to the reins.   1575
At Valencia's main gate, where it was safest,
in front of his wife and daughters
he wanted to put on a show of arms.

The ladies received with great honor,
Bishop Don Jerónimo went on ahead,
dismounted his horse and headed for the chapel   1580.
With the clerics who were there to pray the hours,
dressed in surplice, with silver crosses
they went out to welcomed the ladies and the good Minaya.
The Cid himself does not delay.
He puts on a tunic, he of the long flowing beard.
They saddle and caparison Babieca.   1585
My Cid rides forth
armed with jousting weapons.

Babieca's first charge is so furious
that everyone there is astounded. His name   1590
from that day forth was known to all of Spain.
At the end of their run the Cid dismounted
and went to his wife and children.

When Doña Ximena met him, she threw herself at his feet.
"Thanks, Campeador, who girded your sword
in a fortunate hour!   1595
You have saved me from all kinds of shame.
Here I am, lord, I and your little daughters.
With God's help and yours, they are good girls
and well cared for."

He hugged his wife and daughters tight
while all of them wept for happiness.   1600

All of his vassals were overjoyed.
They celebrated by holding jousts
and tilting at targets.

Hear what he said, who was born in a fortunate hour:
"You, my beloved, honored wife,
and both my daughters, my heart and soul,   1605
come with me into the city of Valencia.
This is the home that I have won for you."

Mother and daughters kissed his hands
and they entered Valencia with the greatest honor.

87. A VIEW OF VALENCIA

My Cid took them straight to the castle 1610
where they ascended to the highest spot.
Their beautiful eyes took in everything:
All of Valencia lay before them,
and, on the other side, the sea.
They see the wide expanse of farms and gardens. 1615
Raising their hands, they give thanks to God
for this vast and beautiful possession.

My Cid and his company live in peace and pleasure.
Winter is over, spring has just begun.

Now I shall give you the news from beyond the sea 1620
about a King Yúsuf who lived in Morocco.

88. YÚSUF SETS OUT FOR VALENCIA

The king of Morocco was angry at the Cid.
"By force he has thrust himself into my lands,
and gives thanks to no one but Jesus Christ."
The king of Morocco gathered his forces. 1625
Fifty times a thousand strong, they took to the sea in ships.
They seek out Valencia, they seek my Cid.
When the ships arrive, they disembark.

89.

Arrived at Valencia, ruled now by Rodrigo, 1630
the unbelievers set up camp and pitched their tents.
News of this comes to my Cid.

90. The Cid Rejoices

"Thanks be to God, the Heavenly Father!
All my worldly good is here with me.
I fought hard to win Valencia, my inheritance. 1635
I will not leave it while I live.

"Thanks to the Creator and Santa María
I have my wife and daughters here.
Now this delicious chance
has come from across the sea.
I will take up arms—indeed, I must. 1640
My wife and daughters shall see me fight.
They can see how we make our homes
in these foreign lands. With their own eyes
they will see how we earn our bread."

To the castle's top he took his wife and children.
Raising their eyes, they saw where the tents were pitched. 1645
"What is this, my Cid? May God protect you!"

"Do not worry, my noble wife.
These are marvelous riches come to us.

You've hardly arrived, and already
they're eager to give you presents!
Your daughters are ready to marry—here's their dowry!"   1650

"I thank you, My Cid, and the Heavenly Father."

"My wife, wait here in this palace, in the castle.
Don't be afraid to watch me fight.
By the grace of God and Our Mother Santa María
my heart grows greater since you are here.   1655
God willing, I'll win the victory tomorrow."

91. The drums of the Moors

No sooner has dawn appeared in the Moorish camp
than their drums begin to thunder.
My Cid rejoices: "What a great day this is!"

His wife is afraid, her heart beats as if to break.   1660
The same with her ladies and daughters—
they have never known such terror since they were born.

Stroking his beard, the Cid said,
"Have no fear, for all this is in your favor!
Before two weeks, God willing,   1665
I'll bring those drums back here for you to look at.
Then they'll go to Bishop Don Jerónimo as trophies
to hang up in Santa María, Mother of God."
After the Cid had made this vow
the ladies cheered up and felt more confident.   1670

The Moors from Morocco rode boldly—
they entered the farms and gardens without fear.

92. The first engagement. Plan of battle.

The lookout saw them and rang the bell.
The Cid's men, his vassals, were ready.
They took up arms with a will
and rode forth from the city.   1675

When they met the Moors they attacked at once
and drove them roughly from the farmland,
killing five hundred Moors that day.

93.

All the way back to the tents the chase continued.
Having done much, they headed home.   1680
Alvar Salvadórez, taken captive, was left behind.
Those who eat the Cid's bread returned to him.
They regaled him with tales of the battle he had seen.
My Cid was happy with all they had done.

"Listen, my knights. This is how it must be.   1685
Today was a good day—tomorrow will be better!
Be armed and ready to ride at daybreak.
Bishop Don Jerónimo will say the Mass
and grant us absolution. Then we will mount

and attack them in the name of God
and the Apostle Santiago! 1690
Better to beat them than let them steal our bread!"

To this they said, "With all our love and will!"

Minaya Alvar Fáñez spoke up quickly:
"Since that's how you want it, Cid, grant me this as well.
Give me a hundred and thirty knights to fight with. 1695
When you launch the charge, I'll come in from the other side.
With God's help, one or both of us will succeed."

To this the Cid replied, "I grant it gladly."

94. Don Jerónimo's request

Day has gone, the night has come.
The Christians prepared themselves without delay. 1700
As the cock was crowing before sunrise
Bishop Don Jerónimo sang Mass for them.
Mass sung, he gave them absolution:

"He who dies with his face to the enemy
I absolve from sin, and God will embrace his soul. 1705

"My Cid, who strapped on your sword in a fortunate hour,
I have sung Mass for you this morning.
I ask you one favor, if I may:
Let me strike the first blow of the battle!"

The Campeador said "Here and now I grant it." 1710

95. The Battle Begins

Everyone fully armed, they exit Valencia's towers,
the Cid giving good instructions to his vassals.
They leave capable men to guard the gates.

The Cid leaps onto Babieca,
well armed in every regard. 1715
With their standard in front
they ride forth from Valencia.
Four thousand knights minus thirty
make up the Cid's company.
Gladly they launch their attack
against fifty thousand.

My Cid strikes with his lance
and then employs his sword.
The blood dripping down to his elbows,
he kills more Moors than anyone can count.

Minaya and Alvar Alvarez
attacked from the other side 1720
and, as it pleased the Creator,
before long the Moors were routed.
The Cid struck King Yúsuf three times. 1725
Escaping the sword, Yúsuf rode his horse hard
and holed up in the castle at Cullera.

My Cid and his vassals pursued him there
and turned back happy from the hunt— 1730
Babieca had proved himself from head to tail.

All that booty fell into his hands,
A count was made of the fifty thousand Moors.
Only a hundred and four escaped. 1735
My Cid's men stripped the field:
of silver and gold they found three thousand marks,
and uncounted quantities of other goods.

The Cid and his men are overjoyed
that God has granted them the victory. 1740
After the king of Morocco fled
my Cid left Minaya to count up the spoils.

With a hundred knights he entered Valencia.
Helmet off and hood pulled back,
he was mounted on Babieca, sword raised in his hand. 1745
The ladies were waiting there to greet him.
He reined in his horse and stopped before them.

"I bow to you, ladies. I've won a great prize for you.
While you held Valencia, I was victorious in the field.
This was the will of God and all His saints, 1750
that when you came they gave us so much treasure.

"You see this bloody sword and sweating horse?
It's with these that we conquer the Moors.
Praying that God lets me live a few more years,
you will grow in honor and they will kiss your hands." 1755

My Cid spoke this on horseback.
When he dismounted, the ladies,
the daughters, and the woman of worth
got down on their knees before the Campeador.
"We live in your grace. May you live for many years!" 1760
They returned with the Cid to the palace
and rested with him on rich couches.

"Now, my wife Doña Ximena, haven't you asked for this?
These ladies who serve you so well
I wish to marry with my vassals. 1765
To each I will give two hundred silver marks
so Castile will know who they've been serving.
Your daughters' weddings will come later."

They all jumped up and kissed his hands.
Joy quickly spread throughout the palace, 1770
and as the Cid said, it was done.

Minaya Alvar Fáñez was in the field
with many men, counting and writing.
Between tents and arms and precious clothes
they found so much it was staggering. 1775
I want to tell you most importantly
they couldn't begin to count the horses
running loose without a master.
The Moorish farmers took quite a few.
Still, the Cid's share was fifteen hundred of the best. 1780
If he got so many, you know the others did well too.

So many precious tents and inlaid tent poles
My Cid and his vassals have won!
The king of Morocco's, finest of them all,   1785
was held up by poles wrought with gold.

The Cid ordered the tent to be left standing:
"A tent like that, come from Morocco,
I'd like to send to Alfonso of Castile—   1790
then he'll believe the stories
that the Cid has a thing or two."

With great riches they enter Valencia.
Bishop Don Jerónimo, that worthy priest
who, when he finally finished fighting
could not count the Moors he had killed,   1795
won a magnificent share.
My Cid, from his fifth of the booty,
gave Don Jerónimo a tenth.

96. A Gift for Alfonso

The Christian folk in Valencia are happy
they have so many goods and arms and horses.   1800
Doña Ximena is glad, and her daughters and their ladies,
who consider themselves as good as married.

My Cid doesn't wait for anything:
"Where are you, good knight? Come here, Minaya.
You've earned your share, no need to thank me.   1805
Now take what you want from mine, and leave the rest.

"Tomorrow morning, go without fail
with horses from this fifth of mine,
each with a saddle, reins and sword.　　　　　　　1810
For the love of my wife and daughters
whom he sent here to be happy,
two hundred horses shall go to King Alfonso
so that he shall speak no ill
of him who rules Valencia."

He ordered Pedro Vermúdez to go with Minaya.　　1815
Quickly they left the next day
with two hundred knights in their train
to kiss King Alfonso's hand, bring greetings from the Cid,
and present two hundred horses from their victory.
The Cid pledged to serve him always,
as long as his body had a soul.　　　　　　　　　1820

97.

Leaving Valencia with their bounty, they travel day and night.
Crossing the mountain range between their countries
they begin to ask for Alfonso's whereabouts.　　1825

98.

Passing through the woods and hills and waters
they come to Alfonso's court in Valladolid.
Pedro and Minaya send him word

to prepare to receive their company:
My Cid of Valencia has sent a gift. 1830

99.

You've never seen the king so glad.
He ordered his nobles to mount up quickly,
and he was among the first to ride
to meet the messengers from the Cid.
You know the Infantes of Carrión were there, 1835
and Count García, the Cid's mortal enemy.
Some of them were pleased, and others not.

When they saw the Cid's vassals,
they looked more like an army than an embassy.
King Alfonso quickly crossed himself. 1840

Minaya and Pedro Vermúdez rode ahead.
Dismounting, they fell to their knees,
kissing the ground and both the king's feet.
"Mercy, most honored King Alfonso! 1845
We kiss you for the Cid, the Campeador.
He calls you lord and calls himself your vassal,
holding dear the honor you have done him.
"A few days ago, good King, he won a battle
against King Yúsuf of Morocco, 1850
routing fifty thousand from the field.
The booty was tremendous—
all of his vassals are now rich men.

He sends you two hundred horses
and kisses your hands."

"I accept them with pleasure," King Alfonso said. 1855
"Thank the Cid for the gift he has sent.
The hour will come when I repay him."
This pleased many, who kissed his hands.
But it weighed on Count García. Bitterly angry,
he went aside with ten of his own clan. 1860
"It's incredible how the Cid's honor has grown!
The more he gains, the less for you and me.
Conquering kings as easily
as if he found them dead and stole their horses!
His deeds will make trouble for us." 1865

100.

King Alfonso spoke:
"I thank the Creator and San Isidro of León
for these two hundred horses the Cid has sent.
As my reign goes on, he will do even greater service.
For you, Minaya and Pedro Vermúdez here, 1870
I order your bodies be served with honor, richly dressed
and fitted with arms of your choosing
so that you look fine for the Cid.
It seems to me quite certain 1875
that good will come out of this news."

101. A Marriage Proposal

They kissed his hands and went to their quarters.
He gave orders to meet all their needs.

Now I shall tell of the sons of Carrión.
They took counsel in secret: 1880
"The Cid's affairs are prospering.
Let's ask for his daughters' hands in marriage—
we'll gain in honor and get ahead."

They went to King Alfonso with their request.

102.

"Our King and natural lord, we ask a favor! 1885
If you please, ask the Cid for his daughters for us.
We wish to marry them,
to their honor and our advantage.

The king mulled this over a good long time.
"I banished the Campeador from Castile. 1890
I've treated him badly
while he has done me a great deal of good.
I'm not sure if this proposal will be welcome.
But since you ask me, I will ask him."

The king called in Minaya and Pedro Vermúdez
and took them apart to a corner. 1895

"Hear me, Minaya, and you too, Per Vermúdez.
My Cid the Campeador has served me well.
He has earned, and he shall have, my pardon.
He may come to see me, if it serves his pleasure.

"Here is another message from my court:　　　　　　1900
Diego and Fernando, the Infantes of Carrión,
wish to marry his two daughters.
Be good messengers, I beg you,
and tell the Campeador
that he will grow in honor and prestige
through this match with the sons of Carrión."　　　　1905

Minaya and Pedro Vermúdez promised:
"We will ask as you have told us.
Then the Cid will do what he thinks best."

"Tell Ruy Díaz, born in a fortunate hour,　　　　　　1910
that I will meet him wherever he chooses.
Let him name the place.
I wish to do him all the good I can."

They bade the king farewell and headed home,
back to Valencia with their company.　　　　　　　　1915
When the Cid heard, he quickly mounted
and rode out to greet them.
Smiling, he embraced them both:

"Welcome, Minaya, and you, Per Vermúdez!
Few countries can boast of two such men!　　　　　 1920

What news from my lord King Alfonso?
Was he pleased? Did he accept my gift?"

Minaya said, "Heart and soul
he is pleased, and grants you his love and favor."

"Thanks be to God!" said the Cid. 1925

(THE CID CONSIDERS ALFONSO'S PROPOSAL)

That said, they now began to speak
about the request from King Alfonso
to give his daughters to the sons of Carrión.
How he would rise in nobility, grow in honor,
how the king advised it with all his heart. 1930
When My Cid heard all this,
he thought about it for a good long while.

"I give thanks for this to Christ our Lord.
I was banished and dispossessed.
With great labor I've earned what I have. 1935
I'm grateful to God that the king now favors me
and asks my daughters for the sons of Carrión.
"They're very proud, and members of his court.
Personally, I wouldn't want this marriage.
But since he advises it
who's worth more than we are, 1940
let's talk about it more in private.
May God in heaven show us what is best."

"Besides all this," Minaya said, "Alfonso asks
that you meet with him, anywhere you wish.
He wants to see you and bestow his favor.   1945
Afterwards you can agree on what to do."
The Cid said, "This pleases my heart."

"It's for you to decide," Minaya said,
"where the meeting will be."

"It would not be surprising if King Alfonso   1950
had summoned us to come to him
to do him honor as our king.
But whatever he wants is fine with us.
By the great river Tajo let us meet
at a time of my lord's own choosing."   1955

They wrote the letters, sealed them well
and sent them off with two knights, saying
"What the king wishes, the Campeador will do."

103. Arrangements for the Meeting

They placed the letters before the king.
When he saw them, his heart was pleased.   1960
"Send greetings to the Cid for me.
Let the meeting take place two weeks from now.
If I'm alive, I'll be there without fail."

They returned to the Cid without delay.

Both sides made ready for the meeting. 1965
Who in Castile had ever seen
so many fine mules, smooth-riding palfreys
and swift, steady chargers?
So many bright pennons and good strong lances,
so many shields embossed with gold and silver, 1970
such mantles and furs and silks from Andros?

The king ordered plentiful provisions
to the banks of the Tajo where they would assemble,
for he was bringing a goodly company.

The Infantes of Carrión were overjoyed, 1975
spending their cash and buying on credit,
sure that before long they would gain
all the gold and silver they could wish.

King Alfonso quickly mounts and rides,
with counts and courtiers and a host of vassals. 1980
The Infantes of Carrión bring a large company.
With the king come vassals from León
and Galicia, as well as countless Castilians.
They loosen their reins and head for the meeting place.

104. Reunion with Alfonso

Meanwhile, in Valencia My Cid 1985
also made ready without delay.
So many fat mules and palfreys in their prime,

swift chargers and splendid arms,
rich capes and cloaks and furs,
the humble and great all dressed in brilliant colors.   1990

Minaya Alvar Fáñez and Pedro Vermúdez,
Martín Muñoz and Martín Antolínez, the worthy of Burgos,
Bishop Don Jerónimo, the best of priests,
Alvar Alvarez and Alvar Salvadórez,
Muño Gustioz, that gallant knight,   1995
and Galínd García from Aragón
all got ready to go with the Cid.

The Cid ordered Alvar Salvadórez and Galínd García   2000
to guard Valencia with all their heart,
and all who remained in their care.
The castle doors should not be opened day or night—
within were his wife and daughters
in whom he placed his heart and soul,
as well as the ladies who served them.   2005
Like a good husband, he commanded
that no one leave the castle until he returned.

They spurred and galloped forth from Valencia,
so many warhorses, big and strong and fast.   2010
My Cid won them all in battle—nobody gave them as gifts.
They headed toward their meeting with the king.
King Alfonso arrived a day early.
When they saw the Cid coming
they rode out to receive him with great honor.   2015
When the Cid caught sight of him

he ordered his company to halt
except for a few knights closest to his heart.

He and these fifteen knights dismounted.
As he had already planned, 2020
he got down on his hands and knees
and took the grass of the field between his teeth,
weeping all the while with joy.
He humbled himself before his lord Alfonso
falling like this at his feet. 2025

It grieved King Alfonso to see this.
"Arise, Cid Campeador—
kiss my hands, and not my feet!
Otherwise, you shall not have my favor."

The Cid remained on his knees. 2030
"I ask you a favor, my natural lord!
Grant me your love as I kneel before you
so that all who are present may hear it."

Said the king, "I do so from my heart and soul.
I pardon you, and grant you my love and favor
throughout my realm from this day forward." 2035

"Thank you! I accept this, Alfonso my lord,
with gratitude to God and then to you
and these vassals gathered here around us."
Still kneeling, he kissed Alfonso's hands,
then rose and kissed him on the mouth. 2040

Everyone gathered there was glad
except Alvar Díaz and García Ordóñez.
The Cid said, "I'm grateful to our Creator.
Having my lord Alfonso's favor,
God will defend me by day and by night.   2045
If it please you, my lord, be my guest."

The king said "Today that would not be right.
You have just come and we were here last night.
Be my guest for now, good Campeador
and tomorrow we'll do as you wish."   2050
Kissing his hand, My Cid agreed.
The Infantes of Carrión paid homage to the Cid:
"We bow to you, Cid, born in a fortunate hour!
Whatever we can do for you, we will."

Rodrigo replied, "May the Creator make it so!"   2055

The Cid was King's guest that day,
and pleased Alfonso's heart so well
he could not get enough of his company.
The king could not help staring at his beard,
which had grown so long in so short a time.
Everyone there was in awe of the Cid.   2060

And so the day passed and the night came on.
Next morning, as the sun rose clear
the Cid asked his vassals to prepare a feast
for all the folk gathered there.
My Cid pleased them all so abundantly   2065

that, content and happy, everyone agreed
they had not had a meal like that in many a year.

(ALFONSO AND THE CID DISCUSS THE MARRIAGE)

Next morning as the sun came up
Bishop Don Jerónimo sang mass.
Afterwards, while they were all assembled   2070
the king began to speak:
"Hear me, my vassals, counts, and noble men!
I wish to ask something of the Cid,
may Christ grant that it be for his good.
I ask for your daughters, Doña Elvira and Doña Sol,   2075
to give as wives to the sons of Carrión.
This wedding, I believe, will be one of honor
and advantage. They ask it and I recommend it.
Let everyone here on both sides, yours and mine,
join me in making this request: 2080
Give them to us, my Cid, may God protect you!"

"I don't know if my daughters are ready to marry,"
said the Cid. "They are young yet, their days are few.
The Infantes of Carrión have great renown,
enough for my daughters and those more noble yet.   2085
I sired my children, but you, Alfonso, brought them up
so we are all three in your debt.
In your hands I leave Doña Elvira and Doña Sol.
Give them to anyone you please, I'll be content."

"Thanks," said the king, "to you and all this court."   2090
Then the Infantes of Carrión
rose and kissed the Cid's hands. In front of Alfonso
they and the Cid exchanged their swords.

Alfonso spoke like the good lord he was:
"I thank you, Cid, and most of all thank God   2095
that you have given me your daughters
for the Infantes of Carrión.
I make this marriage with your love and favor,
and may it please God you'll be happy with it.   2100
"I leave in your hands the Infantes of Carrión.
They will go with you, for I must return.
I give them three hundred silver marks
for wedding expenses or what you wish.
Daughters and sons-in-law, they are all your children now.
They will be in your power in Valencia.   2105
Do with them as you will, My Cid."

My Cid received them and kissed Alfonso's hands.
"Many thanks to you, my lord and king.
You have married my daughters, and not I."   2110

The words have been put into place, the homage given.
Next morning at sunrise
everyone was heading home again.
Now the Cid did something that caused a sensation:
so many fat mules and smooth-paced palfreys,
so many rich and costly garments
he gave to whomever would take his gift.   2115
No one was refused whatever he wanted.

The Cid gave away sixty horses.
All who came to the meeting were pleased.
But now night had come
and their thoughts turned homeward. 2120

The king took the Infantes by the hand
and placed them in the power of the Cid.
"These are your sons, since they are your daughters' husbands.
From now on, Campeador, they are in your care."
"I thank you, King, and accept your gift. 2125
May God in heaven reward me for it."

105.

"I ask you a favor, my natural King:
Since you're marrying my daughters at your pleasure,
name someone to give them away for you,
lest any should flatter themselves
that I gave them with my own hand."

The king answered, "Here's Alvar Fáñez. 2135
Let him take them in hand and give them to the Infantes,
as I have done here, as though they were present.
Let him act as their godfather at the wedding
and tell me about it when we meet again."

"I'll be happy to do it," Alvar Fáñez said. 2140

106. Gifts and Partings

So all was arranged with the greatest care.
"Now King Alfonso, my honored lord,
take something of mine from this meeting.
I brought you twenty palfreys, fully furnished,
and thirty chargers with good saddles.
I kiss your hands and beg you to accept them." 2145

Said King Alfonso, "You overwhelm me!
I accept your gift.
May it please the Creator and all His saints
to reward the pleasure you have given me. 2150
"My Cid Ruy Díaz, you have done me great honor.
You have served me well, and I am more than pleased.
As long as I live, you'll get something back from me.
I commend you to our Creator. Now I must leave.
I pray God in heaven turns everything to the best!" 2155

107.

My Cid sprang onto his horse, Babieca.
"I say here in front of Alfonso my King,
whoever wants to come to the wedding
and receive my gifts, ride with me now!
I don't think you will regret it."

You should have seen all his favorite courtiers
saying farewell to Alfonso, kissing his hands:

"Grant us your favor and permission 2160
to go to Valencia with the Cid,
to the wedding of the sons of Carrión
with the Cid's daughters, Doña Elvira and Doña Sol."
This pleased the king and he let them all go,
the Cid's company increasing as his grew less. 2165

A great host leaves with the Campeador.
They head for Valencia, won in a fortunate hour.
To escort the Infantes Don Fernando and Don Diego
they appoint Pedro Vermúdez and Muño Gustioz—
none better in the household of the Cid— 2170
to learn more of their ways and manners.
With the Infantes comes Ansur González,
a blustering man, long of tongue
and short on other things.

They treat the Infantes of Carrión with honor.
At last they approach Valencia, won by the Cid. 2175
The closer they get, the greater is everyone's joy.

The Cid told Don Pedro and Muño Gustioz:
"Find lodging for the Infantes of Carrión
and keep them company. Tomorrow
when the sun is up they will see their brides, 2180
Doña Elvira and Doña Sol."

108. The Cid speaks with Ximena and his daughters

Everyone retired for the night.
My Cid the Campeador went to the castle
where Doña Ximena and his daughters greeted him:
"Welcome Campeador, who strapped on your sword
in a fortunate hour!   2185
May our eyes look upon you for many days!"

"Thank God I've come home, honored lady!
I bring you sons-in-law who will bring us honor.
Give me thanks, daughters—I've married you well!"
His wife and daughters kissed his hands,   2190
as did all the ladies who served them.

109.

"I give thanks to God and to you,
my Cid of the beautiful beard!
Everything you do is for the best.
Your daughters will lack for nothing all their days."

"When you marry us, we will be rich!"   2195

110.

"My wife Doña Ximena, I also give thanks to God.

And my daughters, Doña Elvira and Doña Sol,
by your wedding we will grow in honor.
But you must know the truth—
I did not bring this up myself.

"My lord Alfonso asked and pleaded for you   2200
so urgently with all his heart
there was no way that I could deny him.
I placed you in his hands, my daughters.
Believe me when I tell you this:
It is he who will give you in marriage, not I."

111. The Marriage

Preparations began in the palace.   2205
From the floor up, rich carpets and hangings
were put in place: silken samite, purple satin
and other precious cloths. You would have loved
to revel and feast in that castle!

All of the knights gather quickly.
When the Infantes of Carrión are sent for,   2210
they ride straight to the palace,
arrayed in all their finery.
Dismounting, they walked with great dignity—
God, how quietly they came in!
My Cid and his vassals receive them.
They bow before him and his wife   2215
and take their seats upon an ornate bench.

All the Cid's vassals with courtesy
wait for the Cid to speak.
Rodrigo rises to his feet:

"Well, since we're here to do this,
why should we put it off? 2220
Come here, Alvar Fáñez, whom I dearly love!
Here are my daughters. I put them in your hands.
You know the king has commanded this,
and I will not fail to do what we've agreed.
You give them to the sons of Carrión. 2225
Then comes the blessing, and we'll be done."
Minaya said "I will do so with pleasure."
The girls arose and the Cid placed them in his hands.

Now Minaya addressed the Infantes of Carrión:
"I have before me two brothers. 2230
By the hand of King Alfonso who commands it,
I give you these ladies, both daughters of noble birth,
to take as your lawful wives, with honor and propriety."

Both receive their brides with love and pleasure
then kiss the hands of the Cid and his wife. 2235
This done, they all leave the palace
and go straight to the church of Santa María.
Don Jerónimo quickly dons his vestments
and waits for them by the door.
He gives them their blessings, and Mass is sung. 2240
Leaving the church, they quickly mounted
and headed for the beach outside the city.

What a display of arms and jousting
My Cid and his vassals put on!
Ruy Díaz rode three different chargers,
and he was delighted with all he saw—   2245
his new sons were excellent horsemen.

They returned with the ladies to Valencia
and a splendid celebration in the castle.
The next day the Cid set up seven jousting targets.
They shattered them all before going in to feast.   2250

Fifteen days the festivities lasted.
At last the noble guests began to leave.
My Cid Don Rodrigo loaded them with gifts:
a hundred horses altogether, palfreys, mules, and chargers,   2255
cloaks and furs and other fine garments
and countless quantities of cash.
The Cid's vassals likewise gave from their own goods.
Whoever wanted gifts was well supplied—   2260
the guests went home rich from the wedding.

The guests are departing, saying goodbye to the Cid
and all of the ladies and noblemen.
They leave My Cid and his vassals well content,   2265
praising them highly, as was only right.

Diego and Fernando are overjoyed,
the sons of Count Don Gonzalo.
The guests leave for Castile. The Cid
and his sons-in-law stay in Valencia.   2270

There the Infantes will dwell two years,
all the while showered with love and honor.

Joyful are the Cid and all his vassals.
May holy Mary and our heavenly Father
grant that this marriage please the Cid   2275
and the one who has proposed it!

Here end the verses of this song.
May the Creator and all His holy saints protect you!

Third *Cantar*

112. THE CID'S LION SCARES THE INFANTES

My Cid was in Valencia with all his vassals
and his sons-in-law, the Infantes of Carrión.
Stretched out on a couch, the Cid was sleeping   2280
when, as you shall see, they had a nasty shock—
the lion got loose and escaped from his cage!
Fear ran through the court. The Cid's vassals
grabbed their cloaks and surrounded him on the couch.   2285

Fernando González, Infante of Carrión,
saw nowhere to hide, no open room or castle keep,
and so he crawled under the couch.
His brother Diego ran from the room, crying
"I'll never see Carrión again!"
In terror he hid behind a wine press,   2290
staining his tunic and cloak.

At this moment the Cid awoke
and looked around the couch at his good vassals.
"What's this, my men? What do you want?"

"Ah, my good lord, the lion gave us a fright!"   2295

My Cid got up on his elbow, then stood upright.

Throwing his cloak about his neck,
he strode toward the beast.

The lion, as soon as it saw him, was so ashamed
it bowed its head before the Cid
and touched its muzzle to the ground.
The Cid took him by the scruff of the neck   2300
and led him back to his cage.
Everyone who saw it was in awe
as they returned to the palace from the court.

My Cid asked for his sons-in-law but couldn't find them.
However much they called them, no one answered.   2305
When they finally found them, pale with fear,
you never saw the like of jokes and kidding
running through that court!
The Cid commanded it cease at once.
The Infantes considered themselves insulted
and fiercely resented every word.   2310

113. An Almoravid army arrives

While they were nursing their grievances
an army from Morocco landed
intending to lay siege to Valencia.
Fifty thousand of the grandest tents—
it was King Búcar, whom you have heard of.

114.

The Cid and all his men were glad— 2315
their wealth would increase, thanks to God.
But the sons of Carrión had heavy hearts.
They had no taste for all these Moorish tents.

The brothers went apart and spoke:
"We counted on gains, not losses! 2320
Now we'll have to take part in this battle.
Chances are we'll never see Carrión again.
The daughters of the Cid will be left widows."

Muño Gustioz overheard their talk
and told the Cid about it. 2325
"Your brave sons-in-law are frightened—
on the eve of battle they long for Carrión!
Go comfort them, God help you.
Let them remain at peace and not take part.
Following you we shall conquer,
with help from the Creator." 2330

My Cid Don Rodrigo came out smiling:
"God save you, my sons-in-law, Infantes of Carrión!
You have my daughters, white as the sun, in your arms.
I long for battle, and you for Carrión.
Stay here in Valencia at your ease and pleasure. 2335
I know these Moors,
and with God's help I'll rout them!"

115. Pedro Vermúdez helps out Fernand

[A sheet is missing from the manuscript. The gap is covered by The Chronicle of Twenty Kings:

As they were speaking, King Búcar sent word to the Cid to leave Valencia. If he did, he could go in peace. If not, Búcar would make him pay for everything he'd done. The Cid said to the messenger, "Tell Búcar, that son of my enemy, that before three days I shall do as he demands."

The next day the Cid ordered his men to arms, and they rode out against the Moors. The Infantes of Carrión asked to strike the first blow. After the Cid had his ranks in order, Fernando, one of the Infantes, rode forward to attack a Moor named Aladraf. When the Moor saw him coming, he also charged forward. The Infante, filled with fear, turned his reins and fled, not daring to wait for his foe.

When Pedro Vermúdez, who was nearby, saw this, he attacked the Moor, fought with him and killed him. Then he took the Moor's horse and went after the Infante who was fleeing. "Don Fernando, take this horse and tell everyone you killed the Moor that it belonged to. I will back up your story."

The Infante replied, "Don Pedro Vermúdez, I thank you deeply for what you've said."

The manuscript picks up again:]
"The hour will come when you will be paid back double."

They rode back together, and Don Pedro agreed
when Fernando started boasting of his deed.   2340
The Cid and his vassals were pleased.
"May it please the Father in heaven
that both my sons-in-law prove brave in battle."

As they spoke, the Moors gathered their hosts
and began to beat their drums.   2345
The sound astonished many of the Christians
who had never heard it before.
Most astounded of all were Fernando and Diego,
who wished to be anywhere but here.

Hear what the Cid, born in a fortunate hour, said: 2350
"Hey, Pedro Vermúdez, good cousin!
Take care of Fernando and Diego for me,
my much-loved sons-in-law. With God's help
the Moors will not hold this field."

116. Pedro refuses the Cid's request. Don Jeronimo asks for a favor

"Let me say, Cid, with all due charity,   2355
The Infantes won't have me for a tutor today.
Whoever wants to can look after them.
As for me, I don't really care for them that much.

"I want to attack the front with my men.
You and yours can firmly guard the rear.
If I run into trouble, you can help me out."   2360

At that moment, Alvar Fáñez rode up:
"Hear me, My Cid, oh loyal Campeador!
This battle is in the Creator's hands
and you are worthy to fight for Him.
Command the attack whenever you think best,
and every man will do his duty. 2365
We'll see what God and your good fortune do!"

"Alright. Let's just take it easy," said the Cid.

Here comes Bishop Don Jerónimo, fully armed.
He pulls up before the Cid, that fortunate man.
"Today I have sung you the Mass of the Holy Trinity. 2370
Because of my desire to kill a Moor
I have left my lands and sought you out.
To honor my Order and my own hands
let me be the first in this attack.

My pennon and shield are emblazoned with deer. 2375
God willing, I would like to try them out
both for my own heart's delight
and to better repay you, my Cid.
If you won't grant this favor,
I shall leave your service."

The Cid replied, "Your wish is my pleasure. 2380
There you see the Moors. Attack them!
We'll see from here how the priest fights."

117. The Attack Begins

Don Jerónimo quickly spurred forward
and attacked the Moors on the outskirts of their camp.
By his good luck and the God who loved him   2385
he killed two Moors with the first blows of his lance.
The lance shaft splintered, he laid hands on his sword.

The Bishop showed his mettle—God, how well he fought!
Two down by his lance, five by the sword,
a multitude of Moors surrounded him.   2390
They struck heavy blows, but could not break his armor.

The man born in a fortunate hour watched intently.
He took up his shield and lowered his lance,
set spur to Babieca, his fast charger,
and rode to attack them with heart and soul.   2395

The Campeador broke through the foremost ranks,
unhorsing seven and killing four.
By God's grace, then and there the rout began.

My Cid and his vassals followed in hot pursuit.
You would have seen so many tent cords cut,   2400
tent stakes pulled up, such finely-carved poles
pulled down. The Cid's men
drove the hosts of Búcar from their camp.

118. The Cid pursues King Búcar

They drove them from their tents and chased them down.
You could see so many chain-mailed arms cut off,
so many heads in helmets hit the ground,   2405
horses without riders running wild.
The pursuit went on for seven miles.

My Cid galloped after King Búcar.
"Come back here, Búcar!
You've come from across the sea
to see the Cid, the man with the great big beard.   2410
Let's embrace and be friends!"

Búcar replied, "God confound such friendship!
I see you spurring in pursuit, a naked sword in hand,
and it looks like you want to try it out on me!
But if my horse doesn't slip or fall   2415
you won't catch me before I reach the sea."

"Not true!" the Cid replied.
Búcar's horse had a good long stride
but the Cid's Babieca was gaining on him.
He overtook Búcar three fathoms from the sea.   2420
Raising Colada high, he brought down a furious blow.
Bursting the jewels from Búcar's crest,
he cut the helmet in half
and split his body right down to his belt.

Killing King Búcar from across the sea,   2425

he won his sword Tizón,
worth a thousand golden marks.
Victors in that great and marvellous battle,
My Cid and all those with him gained great honor.

119. THE CID, EXULTING IN VICTORY, PRAISES THE INFANTES

They returned with the spoils they had won
and thoroughly stripped the battlefield.   2430
Back at the camp they found my Cid,
Ruy Díaz the famous Campeador,
bearing two swords that he treasured.
He galloped over the field of slaughter: 2435
His weathered face was bare, his chain mail hood
thrown back, a rumpled cloth cap covering his hair.

Then he saw something that made him glad.
Raising his eyes and looking far ahead
he saw Diego and Fernando coming,   2440
the sons of Count Don Gonzalo.
My Cid was happy, smiling handsomely:
"Come here, my sons-in-law—you are both sons to me!
I know you're well pleased with your fighting.
Good news will be told of you in Carrión   2445
of how we defeated King Búcar.
As I trust in God and all His saints,
we can be proud of this victory today."

From all directions his vassals were returning. 2455
Minaya Alvar Fáñez now arrived, the shield
that hung from his neck all bashed by swords 2450
and countless lance-blows,
none of which had reached him.
Blood dripping down to his elbows,
he had killed twenty Moors or more.

"Thanks be to God, the Father on High,
and to you, Cid, born in a fortunate hour!
You have killed Búcar and we've won the field.
These riches belong to you and your vassals.
And your sons-in-law have proved themselves, 2460
had their fill of fighting with the Moors."

My Cid said, "I am pleased with this.
And if they're good now,
they'll be even better in the future!"
My Cid meant this well,
but the Infantes took it as an insult.

They brought all their spoils back to Valencia. 2465
My Cid and all his men were overjoyed,
for each one's share was six hundred silver marks.
Getting their share and stashing it away,
the Cid's sons-in-law were sure
they would never be lacking for cash. 2470
In Valencia they were well supplied
with spicy food, fine furs, rich cloaks.
My Cid and his vassals were happy.

120.

There was celebration in the court of the Campeador
after they won the battle and killed King Búcar.   2465
The Cid raised his hand and grasped his beard:

"Thanks be to Christ, the Lord of the world!
Now I have seen what I wanted to see:
my two sons-in-law both fighting in the field with me.
Good news of them will go to Carrión—   2480
they have honored themselves and done us much good.

121. Spoils of Battle

"Everyone has won tremendous booty.
Some we have on hand, and some is in safekeeping."
My Cid, who was born in a fortunate hour
ordered that everyone take his proper share,   2485
not forgetting the fifth that was owed to him.
All agreed, and acted accordingly.
To the Cid's fifth fell six hundred horses,
with countless beasts of burden and huge camels.   2490

122.

What incredible spoils the Cid had won:
"I thank God, who is Lord of this world!
Once I was poor, and now I am rich,

for I have lands and goods, and gold and honor, 2495
and the Infantes of Carrión for sons-in-law!
I win battles as it pleases the Creator—
both Christians and Moors are afraid of me.

"There in Morocco, the land of mosques,
they fear I that will take them by surprise
some night—but no, I don't intend to. 2500
I'll stay in Valencia, not seek them out.
But they shall pay tribute, with God's help,
to me or whoever I please."

Great was the rejoicing in Valencia
by the Cid and all his company 2505
for this rout in which they fought with heart.
And great the joy of his two sons-in-law,
for their share of the booty was five thousand marks.
They thought themselves rich, those Infantes of Carrión. 2510

They and the others came to court.
There was the Cid and Bishop Don Jerónimo,
the good Alvar Fáñez, that battling knight
and many more raised in the household of the Cid.
When the Infantes of Carrión came in 2515
Minaya welcomed them for the Campeador:
"Come, cousins—you have added to our honor!"

The Cid was pleased to see them arrive:
"My sons-in-law, here you see my honored wife
and both my daughters, Doña Elvira and Doña Sol, 2520

who embrace you and serve you with all their hearts.
We defeated the Moors in the field
and killed King Búcar, a proven traitor.
Thanks be to Saint Mary, Mother of our Lord
that you have gained in honor from this marriage. 2525
Good news will go back to the land of Carrión."

123. The Infantes devise a plot

The Infante Fernando replied:
"Thanks to the Creator and you, honored Cid,
we now possess wealth beyond measure.
From you comes our honor, for you we have fought. 2530
What's ours is now safely stored away,
and you can take care of the rest."

The vassals of the Cid were smirking—
those who fought hardest or rode in the pursuit
had never once seen Diego or Fernando.
Because of the jokes they were cracking, 2535
mocking the two of them day and night,
the Infantes between them hatched an evil plot.

They went aside to talk.
They were brothers indeed, of one heart.
Of what they plotted, we shall have no part.

"Let's go back to Carrión. We've stayed here far too long. 2540
The wealth we have is so immense,
as long as we live we'll never spend it all.

124.

"Let's ask for our wives from the Campeador,
tell him we'll take them to Carrión
to show them their lands and estates. 2545
Once they're away from Valencia, beyond his power
we can do as we please with them on the road
before they can bring up what happened with the lion.
We are the heirs of the Counts of Carrión!
We'll carry off treasures of tremendous value 2550
and scorn and shame the daughters of the Cid.

"With this wealth we'll be rich men forever.
We can marry the daughters of kings or emperors!
We are the heirs of the Counts of Carrión!
So we shall scorn the daughters of the Cid 2555
before they can bring up what happened with the lion."

After taking counsel, both returned.
Fernando González silenced the court, and spoke:
"May the Creator protect you, Campeador!
May it please Doña Ximena, and you above all, 2560
and Minaya and all who are here:
Give us our wives who have been blessed to us.
We will take them to our lands in Carrión
so that we may give them the estates
that are theirs by marriage and inheritance. 2565
Your daughters shall see what we possess
and that which our children will share."
The Cid, suspecting no harm, replied:

"I give you my daughters, and something of mine as well.
You give them estates in the lands of Carrión.　　　　2570
I give them as dowry three thousand silver marks,
and give you mules and palfreys in their prime
and warhorses, chargers strong and fast
and many garments made of cloth-of-gold.

"I give you two swords, Colada and Tizón—　　　　2575
you well know I won them like a man.
When I give you my daughters, you are both my sons.
When you go, you take my heart-strings with you.

"Let them know in Galicia, Castile, and León
the riches I send off with my sons-in-law.　　　　2580
Take care of my daughters, for they are your wives.
If you treat them kindly, I'll reward you well."

The Infantes of Carrión agreed to everything.
They received the daughters of the Cid
and all the gifts the Cid had granted.　　　　2585
When everything was just the way they wanted,
they ordered it all to be packed and loaded.

Valencia was buzzing with the news:
Everyone took up arms and galloped fast
to see the Cid's daughters off to Carrión.　　　　2590
They were saying goodbye and about to ride
when both sisters, Doña Elvira and Doña Sol,
got down on their knees before the Cid.
"We ask a favor, father, may God protect you!

You begot us and our mother gave us birth. 2595
We kneel before you, our lady and lord.
Now you are sending us off to Carrión
and we must do as you command.
So we ask this mercy of you both:
Please send us messages in our new land." 2600

The Cid hugged and kissed them both.

125.

Their mother embraced them twice over:
"Go, my daughters, and may the Creator protect you!
You have my blessing, and your father's.
Go to Carrión where you are heirs. 2605
As I see it, you are married well."
They kissed their father's and mother's hands
and received their love and blessing.

My Cid and the others are ready to ride,
splendidly decked out with horses and armor. 2610
The Infantes take leave of lovely Valencia,
bid farewell to the ladies and all the company.
Playing at arms, they ride through the farmlands,
everyone happy, My Cid and his men.

The Campeador saw the omens: 2615
these weddings would not be without some stain.
But there was no repenting now
for they were already married.

126. THE CID PARTS FROM HIS DAUGHTERS

"Where are you, my nephew? You, Félez Muñoz!
You are my daughters' cousin, and love them with
all your heart.
I order you to go with them, all the way to Carrión. 2620
You shall see the estates that are given to my daughters
and bring the news back to the Campeador.

Said Félez Muñoz, "This pleases me heart and soul."

Minaya Alvar Fáñez pulled up before the Cid.
"Let's turn back, my Cid, to Valencia. 2625
God willing, we shall visit them in Carrión."

"To God we commend you, Doña Elvira and Doña Sol.
Always act in a way that will make us proud."

"May God make it so!" the sons-in-law replied. 2630

There was great sorrow at their parting,
father and daughters weeping from their hearts,
along with all the knights who were with the Cid.

"Listen, my nephew—you, Félez Muñoz.
Go to Molina and stay the night. 2635
Bring greetings to my friend, the Moor Abengalvón.
Let him receive my sons-in-law the best he can.
Tell him I'm sending my daughters to Carrión.
Whatever they need, let him serve their pleasure

and escort them as far as Medina, for love of me. 2640
I will reward him well for all he does."

They parted, as the nail parts from the flesh.

(The Infantes conspire against Abengalvón)

The Cid turned back toward Valencia.
The Infantes traveled onward, making camp
at Santa María de Alvarazín. 2645
Then they spurred onward as fast as they could
to reach Molina and the Moor Abengalvón.

When the Moor heard of this, it pleased his heart.
He rode out to receive them with great rejoicing.
God, how well he served them, as they pleased! 2650
Next morning he rode along with them,
leading an escort of two hundred knights.

They traversed the mountains of Luzón,
crossed over the Arbuxelo to the Jalón,
and stayed the night at a place called Ansarera.
To the Cid's daughters the Moor gave gifts,
and fine horses to the Infantes of Carrión. 2655
All this for his great love of the Cid.

The Infantes saw what riches the Moor had brought
and began to plot treason between them: 2660

"Now, since we're already planning
to abandon the daughters of the Cid,
if we could kill the Moor Abengalvón
all of his riches would be ours!
We could keep them as surely as our lands in Carrión—
the Cid will never get justice from us." 2665

While the Infantes were hatching their plot
a Moor who spoke Spanish overheard them
and revealed it at once to Abengalvón:
"Alcalde, my lord, be wary of these men—
I heard the Infantes plotting your murder." 2670

127. Abengalvón confronts the Infantes

Abengalvón was a stouthearted man.
With his two hundred knights he came riding,
all fully armed, and halted before the Infantes.
What the Moor had to say did not please them:

"Tell me, what have I done to you, Infantes of Carrión? 2675
I have been serving you faithfully
while you have been plotting my murder!
If not for My Cid of Vivar
I would do something to you
the whole world would hear of!
I would return his daughters to the Cid,
and you two would never again see Carrión. 2680

128. The oak grove of Corpes

"I part with you as evil men and traitors,
and scorn the name of the sons of Carrión!

"I ask your leave, Doña Elvira and Doña Sol.
May God, the Ruler of this world, so order it
that this marriage may be pleasing to the Cid."   2685

This said, the Moor turned away,
crossed the Jalón with a show of arms
and, like the sensible man he was,
went back home to Molina.

The Infantes of Carrión moved on from Ansarera.
Traveling day and night   2690
they passed Atienza on the left, a powerful fort.
Traversing the mountains of Miedes,
spurring through the Montes Claros
on the left they leave Griza, which Alamos settled,
and the caves where he imprisoned Elpha.   2695
Then, to the right, they went by San Estevan farther on.

The Infantes have entered the oak grove of Corpes.
The mountains are high, the tree branches touch the clouds,
and wild beasts wander all around.
They found a clearing with a fresh, clean spring.   2700
The Infantes ordered the tents pitched there
for all their company. They spent the night
embracing their wives with loving words—
promises broken when the sun came up.

They ordered the mules loaded up with treasure 2705
and the tents taken down where they spent the night.
Their household has all gone on ahead.
The Infantes ordered that no one,
man or woman, should stay behind—
except their wives, Doña Elvira and Doña Sol. 2710
They wanted to have them completely at their pleasure.

When all were gone, and only the four remained
the Infantes of Carrión set about their evil deed.

"Believe it, Doña Elvira and Doña Sol—
here in this wilderness you will be scorned and spurned! 2715
Today we'll depart and you will be left behind.
You will have no part in the lands of Carrión.
Then the news will get back to the Cid
that we have avenged our dishonor with the lion."

They stripped off the ladies' furs and cloaks, 2720
leaving them bare but for shifts and slips.
The vile traitors had spurs on their boots,
and hard leather cinch straps in their hands.

When the ladies saw this, Doña Sol spoke up:
"For God's sake we beg you, Diego and Fernando! 2725
You have two swords, strong and sharp,
one named Colada, the other called Tizón.
Cut off our heads and we shall be martyrs.
Moors and Christians both will blame you
for we have done nothing to deserve it. 2730

Do not commit such an outrage upon us!
If you beat us, the shame and dishonor are yours—
they'll condemn you in assemblies and in court."

The ladies' pleading does no good.
The Infantes begin to whip them with flying cinch straps. 2735
Stabbing with sharpened spurs,
they rip through their clothes and flesh.
Clean blood gushes out on the silken slips.
They can feel the pain in their hearts. 2740

How wonderful if, the Creator willing,
the Cid had appeared at that very moment!
They beat them till they were unconscious,
their shifts and slips all soaked with blood.
The Infantes grew tired of hitting them, 2745
competing to see who could deal the hardest blows.

Doña Elvira and Doña Sol were silent.
They left them for dead in the oak grove of Corpes.

129.

They had stripped off their cloaks and their ermine furs
and left them to suffer in their slips 2750
at the mercy of the mountain birds
and the beasts of the wilderness.
Know that they left them for dead.
They did not think they were still alive.
What luck if the Cid had appeared just then!

130. The Infantes boast about their deed

The Infantes left them for dead
in the oak grove of Corpes, 2755
neither able to help the other.
The Infantes praised themselves
as they rode through the woods:

"Now we're avenged for our marriages.
We wouldn't have taken them
even as mistresses, unless they had begged us! 2760
We could never embrace them as equals.
So the dishonor of the lion is avenged."

131. Félez Muñoz finds the daughters

The Infantes went on flattering themselves.
But I want to tell you about Félez Muñoz,
the nephew of the Cid. When the Infantes 2765
told him to go on ahead, he was not happy.
Going down the road, his heart was heavy
and he soon slipped away from the others.

In a thicket he hid himself
until he could see his cousins go by 2770
or find out what the Infantes had done.
He saw the Infantes coming and heard their talk,
but they didn't see or suspect him there—
you know he was a dead man if they did.

The Infantes spurred onward 2775
and Félez went down the trail where they had come.
There he found his cousins, close to death.

Shouting "Cousins! Cousins!" he dismounted,
tied up his horse and attended to them.
"Oh cousins, my cousins, Doña Elvira and Doña Sol! 2780
So this is how the Infantes prove their courage.
May it please God and Santa María
they get a just reward for what they've done!"

He turned them both over
but they were too far gone to speak.
His heartstrings were torn as he pleaded, 2785
"Cousins! Cousins! Doña Elvira and Doña Sol!
Wake up, cousins, for the love of God,
while it's still daylight, before night comes
and the wild beasts devour us in these woods."

Little by little, they came to themselves.
Doña Elvira and Doña Sol both opened their eyes 2790
and saw Félez Muñoz before them.

"Get up, cousins, for the love of the Creator!
When the Infantes see that I'm gone
they'll come looking for me.
If God doesn't help us, we'll die here!" 2795

Through great pain, Doña Sol spoke:
"Cousin, if the Campeador deserves well of you,
bring us water, for the love of God!"

Taking his new hat, fresh from Valencia, 2800
Félez filled it with water and gave it to the ladies.
Deeply wounded, they drank their fill.

At his urging, at last they sat up.
He encouraged and comforted them
until they began to regain their strength. 2805
He mounted the sisters on his horse
and covered them both with his blanket.

Taking his horse by the reins, he led them away.
The three were alone in the forest of Corpes.
Between night and day they came through the mountains 2810
and down to the waters of the Duero.
He left them at the tower of Urraca.

Félez Muñoz pushed on to Sant Estevan
where he found Diego Téllez, a vassal of Alvar Fáñez.
When Diego heard the news, it grieved his heart. 2815
He rounded up mounts and fine garments
and went to get Doña Elvira and Doña Sol.
Diego brought them back to Sant Estevan
and did them all the honor that he could.
The folk of Sant Estevan have always had good sense. 2820
When they heard the news it weighed heavy on their hearts.
They nursed the Cid's daughters back to health,
and there they stayed until they were well again.

(The Cid and Alfonso hear the news)

While the Infantes continued to praise themselves,
their deed would deeply grieve good King Alfonso. 2825

The news has arrived in Valencia.
When they tell my Cid the Campeador
he sits for a long time, deep in thought.
He raises his hand and grasps his beard:

"Thanks be to Christ, who is Lord of the world 2830
for this honor the sons of Carrión have done me!
By this beard, which no one has ever pulled,
they won't get away with this.
And I will marry my daughters better!"

It grieved My Cid and all his court 2835
and Alvar Fáñez, heart and soul.
Minaya rode out with Pedro Vermúdez
and Martín Antolínez, the good man of Burgos
and two hundred knights. The Cid commanded
them to ride both day and night
and bring his daughters back to Valencia. 2840

They don't delay to carry out his orders.
Quickly they mount and, riding night and day
come to Gormaz, a very strong castle.
There, truth be told, they rested for a night.

To Sant Estevan the news arrives 2845

that Minaya will be coming for his cousins.
Like worthy men, those of Sant Estevan
receive Minaya and all his knights.
That evening they gave great tribute to Minaya.
He did not wish to take it, but it pleased him well. 2850

"Thanks for this honor, men of Sant Estevan,
knowing as you do what has happened to us.
The Cid gives you thanks from where he is,
just as I do from here. I know
that God in heaven will reward you well." 2855

Everyone thanked him and, well pleased
each headed to bed for the night.
Minaya went to see where his cousins were.
When both of them saw him, they said:

"We're as glad to see you as we would be the Creator! 2860
Give thanks to Him that we're still alive.
In the days to come, when we're at leisure
we'll tell you everything that happened."

132. The daughters return to Valencia

The ladies and Alvar Fáñez wept,
and Pedro Vermúdez as well, who said:

"Doña Elvira and Doña Sol, don't worry— 2865

now you're alive and well and safe from harm.
You've lost a good marriage, but you'll get a better one.
And we shall see the day when we avenge you!"

They spent the night contentedly
and were ready to ride the next morning.   2870
Sant Estevan's men escorted them,
keeping them company
as far as the Rio de Amor
where they bade them farewell and turned back.

Minaya and the ladies pressed ahead.
They crossed the Alcoceva, leaving Gormaz on the right,   2875
went by the place called Bado de Rey
and reached Berlanga, where they spent the night.

In the morning they rode again
and came to rest at Medinaceli.
Next day they made it to Molina.   2880
This pleased the Moor Abengalvón
who joyfully rode out to meet them.
For his love of the Cid
he gave them a sumptuous dinner.

At last they were headed for Valencia.
When the news reached the Campeador   2885
he quickly rode out to welcome his daughters,
whirling his sword for joy.
With a big smile he hugged and kissed them both.

"Welcome, my daughters! God keep you from harm! 2890
I accepted this marriage; I did not dare oppose it.
May it please the Creator in heaven
that I see you better married in the future.
God grant me vengeance on my sons-in-law from Carrión!"

The daughters kissed their father's hands. 2895
With a great show of arms they entered the city.
Doña Ximena was overjoyed to see them.

The man born in a fortunate hour wastes no time.
He holds a private meeting with his men
and plans to send a message to Alfonso. 2900

133. The Cid asks Alfonso for Justice

"Where are you, Muño Gustioz, my worthy vassal?
In a fortunate hour I raised you in my court!
Take this message to Alfonso of Castile.
Kiss his hand for me with heart and soul,
for I am his vassal and he is my lord. 2905

"Tell him of this dishonor
the Infantes of Carrión have done me,
which will grieve the good king's heart.
He married my daughters, for I did not give them away.
When they left my daughters dishonored,
though some of the shame is on us, 2910
the greater part falls upon him.

"They have taken off much of my treasure,
which I count with the other dishonor.
Let him call them to court for me
or some other meeting or assembly
where I can get justice from the Infantes, 2915
so great is the rancor in my heart."

Muño Gustioz galloped off
with two knights to attend him
and squires from the household of the Cid.
They rode from Valencia fast as they could, 2920
resting neither day nor night.
They found King Alfonso in Sant Fagunt.
He is King of Castile and King of León
and of the Asturias and San Salvador.
As far as Santiago he is lord: 2925
the Counts of Galicia count him as their master.

As soon as Muño Gustioz dismounted
he kneeled before the saints and prayed to God.
Then he headed for the palace and the court
with his two knights who guard him as their lord. 2930

As soon as he entered the court
the king saw him and recognized him.
Alfonso rose and received him warmly. Muño Gustioz
got down on his knees and kissed the king's feet. 2935
"Your grace, King Alfonso, ruler of many realms!
The Cid kisses your hands and feet,
for he is your vassal and you are his lord.

"You married his daughters to the sons of Carrión.
This was an honor you wished for us.   2940
Now you know what kind of honor they brought us—
how the Infantes of Carrión insulted us,
brutally beating the daughters of the Cid,
stripping and lashing them to their great shame,
leaving them helpless in the oak grove of Corpes   2945
for the wild beasts and birds of prey to find.

"His daughters are back in Valencia now.
He kisses your hand as a loyal vassal
and asks that you bring the Infantes to trial or court.
He considers himself dishonored, and you still more so,   2950
and knows this will grieve you, for you are wise.
Let My Cid have justice from the sons of Carrión!"

For a long time the king pondered silently.
"I tell you truly that this grieves my heart.
And what you've said is true, Muño Gustioz—   2955
for I married his daughters to the sons of Carrión.
I did it with good intentions, for his benefit.
I wish now they'd never been married!

"Both I and the Cid have heavy hearts.
As I hope for salvation, I'll help him get justice.   2960
I haven't done this for a long, long time
but my heralds will travel throughout the realm
announcing a court to be held in Toledo.
My counts and nobles all will come.
I'll command the Infantes of Carrión to be there   2965
and give justice to my Cid the Campeador.

134. King Alfonso calls everyone to court

"He shall have no grievance left, if I can help it.
Tell the Cid, born in a fortunate hour
to be ready with his vassals
to come to Toledo in seven weeks—
this is the term I allow him.   2970
I'm holding this court out of love for the Cid.
Greet everyone for me and tell them to take comfort:
what they have suffered shall add to their honor."

Muño Gustioz said goodbye
and went back to my Cid.

Just as he promised, Alfonso of Castile
took on this business without delay.   2975
He sent letters to León and Santiago,
to the Galicians and Portuguese,
to the Castilians and those in Carrión
that he would hold court in Toledo.   2980
In seven weeks' time they must assemble there—
those who did not would no longer be his vassals.
Throughout his realm it was understood
no one must disobey the king's command.

135. Arrivals at the court

The court the king is holding

weighs heavy on the Infantes of Carrión.　　　　　2985
They are afraid my Cid the Campeador will come.
They ask advice from all their relatives
and beg the king to excuse them from this court.

"By God, I will not!" said the king.　　　　　　　2990
"My Cid the Campeador is coming
and I shall give him justice
for he has a grievance against you.
Whoever does not attend my court
must leave my kingdom, for he will lose my favor."

Now the Infantes see they must obey.　　　　　　2995
They take counsel with all their family.
Count Don García, who hated the Cid
and always sought to harm him,
took part and gave them his advice.

The appointed time came, and they went to court.　3000
The first one to come was the good King Alfonso
with Count Henry and Count Raymond,
the father of the Emperor,
Count Fruella and Count Birbón.
Many men learned in law came too,　　　　　　　3005
all of the best from Castile.

Count García came with the Infantes of Carrión,
also Ansur González and Gonzalo Ansúrez.
Diego and Fernando both were there
with a great band of henchmen,　　　　　　　　　3010
planning to put the Cid to shame.

They were gathered from everywhere,
but the Campeador had not yet come.
The king was not pleased with his delay.
But on the fifth day the Cid arrived, 3015
sending Alvar Fáñez ahead
to kiss the king's hands and assure him
that the Cid was coming soon.
The king's heart was glad at hearing this.
With many knights he mounted up 3020
and rode out to receive him.

The Cid and his men came well prepared,
a fitting company for such a lord.
When he caught sight of good King Alfonso,
the Cid got down on the ground 3025
intending to humble himself before his lord.

When the king saw this, he hurried forward:
"By Saint Isidore, we'll have none of that!
Mount up, my Cid, or I shall be displeased.
Let's greet each other heart and soul. 3030
What weighs upon you hurts my heart as well.
God grant the court will do right by you today."

"Amen," said my Cid the Campeador
kissing the king's hand, then embracing him.
"I thank God to see you, my lord. 3035
I humbly bow to you and Count Raymond
and Count Henry and everyone here.
God save our friends, and most of all you, my lord!

"My wife Doña Ximena, that worthy woman
kisses your hands, along with both of my daughters.   3040
We hope you are grieved by what happened to us."

"May God save me, I am!" said the king.

136.

The king turned his horse toward Toledo,
but the Cid did not want to cross the Tajo tonight.
"A favor, my King, may God save you!   3045
While you return to the city,
I and mine will sleep at San Serván.
The rest of my company will arrive tonight.
We will hold vigil in that sacred place
and enter the city tomorrow.   3050
I will come to court before I break my fast."
The king said, "I am pleased with this."

King Alfonso returned to Toledo.
My Cid stayed in San Serván.
He had them place candles upon the altar: 3055
he wished to keep vigil in this holy place,
praying and talking to God in private.

Minaya and the good men with him
were ready when the morning came.

137. The Cid's men prepare, expecting treachery

They said matins and prime towards dawn. 3060
The Mass was done before the sun came up,
and all had made generous offerings.

"You, Minaya Alvar Fáñez, my good right arm,
will go with me, and Bishop Don Jerónimo,
with Pedro Vermúdez, Muño Gustioz, 3065
Martín Antolínez, the worthy man of Burgos,
Alvar Alvarez, Alvar Salvadórez,
Martín Muñoz, born in a lucky hour,
and my nephew, Félez Muñoz.
Mal Anda, the learned lawyer, will also come, 3070
and Galínd García of Aragón.
Along with these, make up a hundred
from all my good men here.
"Wear padded tunics to support your war gear,
and shirts of chain mail brilliant as the sun.
But cover them with coats of fur and ermine, 3075
and tie the laces tight to hide your armor.
Under your cloaks, carry swords both sweet and sharp.

"This is the way I will go to court
to demand my rights and speak my reason.
If the Infantes of Carrión come looking for trouble, 3080
with a hundred men like this I'll have no fear."

Everyone said, "So be it, lord,"
and prepared themselves just as he said.

The Cid wasted no time in getting ready.
Pulling good cloth stockings on his legs,   3085
he slipped on his tooled-leather shoes.
His finely-woven shirt, white as the sun
was fitted with gold and silver fastenings
and tailored cuffs that fit him perfectly.

Next came a gold-embroidered silken tunic,   3090
then a robe of red leather fringed with gold
that the Cid wore wherever he went.
For his head, a hood of fine linen
woven with golden threads,
made so that no one could pull his hair.
Likewise, he bound up his long beard with a cord
to prevent any possible insult to his person.
Over it all went a precious mantle.
No one could take their eyes off the man.   3100
With the hundred he had ordered to get ready
he mounted and galloped away from San Serván.

(THE CID ENTERS THE COURT)

The Cid arrived, ready for the court.
Dismounting at the outer gate
they entered with a somber air,   3105
my Cid surrounded by his hundred men.

When they saw the Cid enter
good King Alfonso rose to his feet

along with Counts Henry and Raymond
and after them all the others,   3110
receiving the Cid with great honor.
But García Ordóñez would not rise,
nor anyone with the Infantes of Carrión.

The king said to the Cid:
"Come here, my Campeador
and sit on this bench which you once gave me.   3115
Though some may resent it,
you are a better man than we are."

The man who conquered Valencia thanked the king:
"Remain in your seat, my King and lord.
I shall stay here with my men."
The Cid's reply warmed the king's heart.   3120
The Cid seated himself on a lathwork bench
while his hundred men stood all around him.
Every eye was fixed upon the Cid
with his long beard tied up in a cord.
Everything about him spoke of manhood.
The Infantes alone could not meet his gaze, for shame.

(KING ALFONSO OPENS THE PROCEEDINGS)

Alfonso rose to his feet once more:
"Hear me, my vassals. May the Creator bless you!
Since I became King, I've held only two courts:
one in Burgos, the other in Carrión.   3130

I have come to Toledo today
for love of my Cid, who was born in a fortunate hour
to give him justice from the Infantes of Carrión.

"They have done him a great wrong, as everyone knows.
Counts Henry and Raymond shall act   3135
as judges in this case, along with all the other Counts
who don't belong to either side.
All of you put your minds to this,
well-versed in the law as you are,
and find what is right
for I shall approve no wrong.

"Let both parties keep the peace today.
I swear by San Isidro, whoever disturbs my court   3140
shall leave my kingdom and lose my love.
I will side with whoever is in the right.

"Now let My Cid make his demands
and we'll see how the sons of Carrión reply."

(THE CID MAKES HIS FIRST DEMAND)

My Cid rose and kissed the king's hands.   3145
"I thank you, my lord and King,
for calling this court in my honor.
Here is what I demand from the Infantes of Carrión.
By their leaving my daughters, I am not dishonored.
You married them yourself, my King,
and you will know what to do about it now.   3150

"When they took my daughters,
whom I loved with my heart and soul,
I gave them the swords Colada and Tizón.
I won them like a man, and wished for the Infantes
to honor themselves and serve you well with them.   3155

"When they left my girls in the oak grove of Corpes
they cut all ties with me and lost my love.
Let them give me back my swords,
now they're no longer my sons-in-law."
The judges granted the justice of his plea.

Count Don García said, "We'll talk it over."

(The Infantes are relieved at this modest request)

The Infantes of Carrión now stepped aside   3160
with all their relatives and followers.
Quickly they came to agreement on the plea.
"The Cid has done us an enormous favor,
not claiming the dishonor of his daughters!   3165
We can settle that matter easily with Alfonso.
Let's give him the swords and be done with it.
Once he has them, the court will adjourn
and the Cid will have no more claims upon us."

After this parlay, they returned to court.   3170

"Your grace, King Alfonso, our lord!
We cannot deny the Cid gave us two swords.
Since he demands and desires them,
we wish to return them in your presence."

They took the swords, Colada and Tizón   3175
and placed them in the hands of King Alfonso.
He drew the swords—
they blazed throughout the court,
their hilts and guards of solid gold.
Everyone marveled at the sight.

The Cid received them, kissed Alfonso's hands   3180
and returned to the bench he had risen from.
Holding them up in his hands, he gazed upon them.
They could not have been switched, for he knew them well.
His whole being rejoiced. He smiled with all his heart.

The Cid raised his hand and stroked his beard.   3185
"By this beard, that no one has ever pulled,
these swords will avenge my daughters,
Doña Elvira and Doña Sol!"

He called to his nephew, Pedro Vermúdez.
Extending his hand, he gave him the sword named Tizón.
"Take her, nephew—she now has a better master."   3190

To Martín Antolínez, the worthy man of Burgos,
he held out his hand with Colada.
"Martín Antolínez, my worthy vassal,

take Colada. I won her from a noble master,
Count Ramón Berenguer of Barcelona.   3195
I commend her to your care
knowing that when the occasion arises
you will win great honor with her."
Martín kissed his hand and took the sword.

(The Cid demands his money back)

The Cid rose to his feet once more.
"Thanks to the Creator and you, my King,   3200
I've received satisfaction for my swords, Colada and Tizón.
I have another grievance with the Infantes.
When they took my daughters from Valencia
I gave them three thousand marks of gold and silver.
Even after I did this, they still carried out their plans.   3205
Give me my money—you're no longer my sons-in-law!"

You should have heard the Infantes of Carrión complain!
Count Raymond addressed them: "Say yes or no."

The Infantes of Carrión replied,
"We've already given the Cid his swords   3210
to settle this claim. He asked for no more,
so this case is finished."

"If it please the king, this court has decided
that they shall satisfy the Cid's demands."

The king said, "I give my assent."

The Campeador came to his feet: 3215
"The money I gave you, either give it back
or justify what you've done!"

The Infantes and company step aside again.
They can't reach agreement, for the sum is great
and the sons of Carrión have spent it all.

Returning to court, they complain to the king,   3220
"The man who won Valencia
is now putting the squeeze on us!
So great is his lust for our riches
we'll have to pay with estates in Carrión."

When they finished their plea, the judges said,
"If this pleases the Cid, we won't oppose it.   3225
But as for our verdict, we order the money
must be paid right here in court."

At this point King Alfonso spoke:
"We all know what the Cid demands is just.   3230
Of the three thousand marks I have two hundred
given me by the Infantes of Carrión.
I shall give it back, since they lack money,
so they can give it to the Cid.
I don't want to keep what they owe to him."   3235

Fernando González said, "We have no cash."

Count Raymond responded:
"Since you have spent the gold and silver,
we give this judgment before the king:
pay it in goods that the Cid will accept."   3240

Now the Infantes saw what they had to do.
You would have seen them lead in so many chargers,
fat mules and seasoned palfreys,
so many good swords and armor and accoutrements.
The Cid accepted it all   3245
at the value placed upon it by the court.

All but the two hundred marks Alfonso had
the Infantes had to borrow to pay the Cid,
for their own wealth was not sufficient.
You know they got the worst of that transaction.

138. THE CID CHALLENGES THE INFANTES

The Cid has accepted their goods   3250
and his men taken care of them.
But when that business was done
he brought up one final thing:

"A favor, my lord and king, for the love of charity!
I cannot forget the greatest grievance of all.
Let all the court hear me and feel my pain.   3255
The Infantes of Carrión have done me such vile dishonor
I cannot let them go without a challenge.

139.

"Tell me, Infantes of Carrión:
What have I done to deserve this from you,
in truth or in jest, or for any reason?
I will make it up to you, before this court.

"Why did you tear the fabric of my heart? 3260
When you left Valencia, I gave you my daughters
with every honor and abundant wealth.
If you didn't want them, you treacherous dogs,
why did you take them from Valencia?
Why did you strike them with cinches and spurs? 3265

"You left them alone in the oak grove of Corpes
for the wild beasts and birds of prey.
You are dishonored for what you have done.
If you won't give me satisfaction, let the court decide."

140. THE CID DEFENDS HIS HONOR AND HIS BEARD

Count Don García got to his feet. 3270
"Your grace, oh King, the best in all of Spain!
The Cid has prepared himself for this court
by growing his beard and wearing it long,
shocking some and striking fear in others!

"The Infantes of Carrión have such noble birth 3275

they shouldn't want the Cid's daughters even as concubines!
So who gave them as spouses and wives?
They have done right to leave them as they did.
We care nothing for what the Cid says."

At this, my Cid grasped his beard and answered: 3280
"Thank God who rules heaven and earth, this beard
is long because it grew at its own pleasure.
What right have you, Count, to accuse my beard?
It has grown freely from the very start.
No son of woman has ever pulled it, 3285
no Moor or Christian has ever torn it out—
the way I did to yours at the castle of Cabra!
When I took Cabra and took you by the beard,
there was not a lad who didn't pluck out a pinch.
The part I pulled out hasn't grown back yet!" 3290

141. Fernando scorns the daughters of the Cid

Fernando González jumped up shouting—
listen to what he said:

"Enough of that, Cid! Let go of this argument.
We've paid you back what is yours.
Don't stir up more trouble between us. 3295

"By birth we are from the Counts of Carrión!
We should marry the daughters of kings or emperors,

not the children of petty knights.
We did right to leave your daughters.
Know this: our honor is not less now, but greater!" 3300

142.

My Cid looks at Pedro Vermúdez:
"Speak up, Mute Pedro, man of few words!
My daughters are your first cousins.
When they say this to me
they're slapping your face as well!
If I answer this challenge myself
you won't have a chance to defend them." 3305

143. Pedro Vermúdez replies to Fernando

Pedro Vermúdez tries to speak.
His tongue is tied at first,
but once he starts he doesn't hesitate:

"You have gotten into the habit, Cid,
of calling me 'Pedro the Mute' at every meeting. 3310
You know I can't help my speech,
but when it comes to deeds I shall not fail.

"You lie, Fernando, in everything you say!
You grew in honor through the Campeador.

"I can tell you a thing or two about yourself.   3315
Remember when we fought at Valencia?
You asked for the honor of first blood from the Cid.
Seeing a Moor, you rode out to meet him,
but turned and fled before he could reach you.
If I hadn't helped out, he would have done you harm.
But I passed you and met with the Moor,   3320
defeating him with the first few blows.

"I gave you his horse and kept it a secret—
until this day I've never told a soul.
In front of the Cid and his men you bragged
how you'd killed the Moor and done a manly deed.   3325
They all believed you—no one ever knew the truth.
You're a pretty fellow, but a craven coward.
Tongue without hands, how dare you speak!
"Tell me, Fernando, and admit the truth:
Does the incident with the lion come to mind,   3330
when my Cid was asleep and the beast got loose?
And you, Fernando, what did you do in your fear?
You hid behind the couch of the Campeador!
You crawled under the couch, Fernando,
and today you are worth less because of it.

"We stood around the couch to protect our lord   3335
until the Cid, the man who won Valencia, awoke.
He rose from the couch and walked toward the lion
which bowed its head and waited for the Cid.
It let him take it by the neck and put it in its cage.

"When the Campeador came back   3340
he saw all his vassals gathered round.
But when he asked for his sons-in-law
they were nowhere to be found.

"I defy you as a villian and a traitor!
I will fight here before King Alfonso
for the sake of the Cid's two daughters,
Doña Elvira and Doña Sol.
By deserting them you lost your honor.
They are women and you are men,
but they are worth more in every way than you.

"When we meet in combat, if it please the Creator
you will confess yourself a traitor   3350
and everything I've said will be proven true."
There the case rested between them.

145. Martín Antolínez answers Diego's challenge

Now hear what Diego González said:
"We come from the purest blood of Counts.
We should never have made these marriages   3355
or mixed our blood with Ruy Díaz of Vivar.
We don't regret abandoning your daughters.
No, it is they who will sigh their whole lives long.
What we did to them
will always be thrown in their faces.
I will defend this against the bravest man—
that we have gained honor by leaving them!"   3360

146

Martín Antolínez rose to his feet.
"Shut up, you traitor, mouth without truth!
Let's not forget the matter of the lion:
You ran out the door and hid in the corral,
squeezing yourself behind the winepress. 3365
You've never worn that cloak or tunic since!

"I'll fight for this, I will not let it pass:
Because you abandoned the daughters of the Cid,
they are worth more than you in every way.
When the fight is done, you'll confess with your own mouth 3370
that you are a traitor and all you've said is lies."
And there the case rested between them.

147. Ansur González ridicules the Cid

Ansur González barged into the palace
dragging his tunic and ermine cloak.
His face was red from feasting 3375
and there was little sense in what he said:

148.

"Now men, who ever saw such a terrible thing?
Whoever heard of this Cid from Vivar?
Let him go back to the river Ovirna,
to sharpen his millstones

and collect his cornmeal, the way he used to do! 3380
Who gave him the right to marry the Carrións?"

149. Muño Gustioz challenges Ansur

Now Muño Gustioz got up:
"Shut your mouth, you despicable traitor!
You always break fast before you go to prayers
so when you give people the kiss of peace
you fill everyone around you with disgust. 3385

"You never speak truth to friend or lord—
false to all, and most of all to God.
I want no part of your friendship.
I'll make you admit that you are what I say you are!"
"The case is now closed," King Alfonso said. 3390
"Those who have issued challenges shall fight.
May God save us!"

(Two princes ask a favor of the Cid)

No sooner had the case been closed
than two caballeros appeared in the court,
one named Ojarra, the other Iñigo Jiménez.
One came from the prince of Navarra,
the other from the prince of Aragón. 3395

They kissed the hands of King Alfonso

and asked for the daughters of my Cid,
that he might give them the honor and blessing
to be queens of Navarra and Aragón.

The court went silent, waiting for the answer. 3400
My Cid the Campeador arose.

"Your grace, King Alfonso, for you are my lord!
I give thanks to God that Navarra and Aragón
have asked me for my daughters. 3405
You married them before, not I.
Now I place my daughters in your hands.
I will do nothing without your command.
The king rose and called for silence.
"I beg you, most excellent Campeador 3410
to give your consent to this marriage,
which I now authorize in this court,
for it will enlarge your name and lands and honor."

The Cid rose and kissed the king's hands.
"Since it pleases you, I grant it, lord." 3415

"God reward you for this," said the king.

"To you, Ojarra, and you, Iñigo Jiménez
I grant permission for this marriage
of the Cid's daughters, Doña Elvira and Doña Sol
with the princes of Navarra and Aragón, 3420
celebrated with honor and with blessing."

Ojarra and Iñigo Jiménez arose,
kissed the hands of King Alfonso
and then of my Cid the Campeador.
They paid homage and gave solemn oaths   3425
that all would be as they said, or better.
Many in the court were pleased—
but not the Infantes of Carrión.

(MINAYA ASKS FOR ONE LAST WORD)

Minaya Alvar Fáñez now stood up.
"I ask your grace as King and lord,   3430
and may it not displease the Cid.
Having heard you all speak in court,
I would like to say a bit myself."
The king said, "That's fine with me, Minaya.
Say what you wish."   3435

"I beg you all to hear me in this court,
for I have a great grievance against the Infantes.
I gave them my cousins at the king's command.
The Infantes received them with honors and blessings.
The Cid gave them a great deal of wealth   3440
and yet they abandoned them, to our sorrow.

"I challenge their bodies as villains and traitors!
By birth you come from the Beni-Gómez,
a line of Counts of worth and valor,
but we know how well you have behaved.   3445

"I thank the Creator the princes of Navarra and Aragón
have asked for my cousins, Doña Elvira and Doña Sol.
Once they were yours, to hold in your arms.
Now you must kiss their hands and call them "My Lady".   3450
You must serve them, no matter how little you like it.

"Thanks be to God and King Alfonso
My Cid's honor has increased so much!
Infantes, you are everything I say you are,
and if anyone wants to deny it,   3455
I am Alvar Fáñez, a better man than you are!"

Gómez Peláyet got up. "Minaya, what use is all this talk?
There are plenty of men in this court who could take you on.
He who says otherwise does so at his danger.
If, God willing, we come out well from this,   3460
then we'll see whether what you've said is true."

(Arrangements for the trial by combat)

The king said, "Enough of this.
Let no one make any further accusations.
The combat will take place tomorrow at dawn,   3465
three against three who challenged in the court."

Then spoke the Infantes of Carrión:
"Give us some time, good King. It cannot be tomorrow,
for the Cid has our horses and armor.
First we must go to our lands in Carrión."   3470

The king said to the Cid,
"You choose the place for the combat."

The Cid said, "I will not choose,
for I wish to return to Valencia, not go to Carrión."

The king said, "As you wish, Campeador.   3475
Give me your champions, fully armed,
and let them go with me. I will be their protector,
watching over them as a lord does a good vassal
so they suffer no harm from any Count or knight.

"Here I set a fixed date in this court: 3480
In three weeks, in the fields of Carrión
this combat shall take place before me.
Whoever does not come shall lose his case
and be declared defeated and a traitor."   3485
My Cid kissed his hands and said, "This pleases me.
My three knights are now in your keeping.
I commend them to you as my lord and King.
They are prepared to do all they need to do.
Return them with honor to me in Valencia
for the love of God!"   3490

The king replied, "May God grant it!"

(The Cid unbinds his beard and says goodbye)

With this, the Cid pulled back his hood
of fine cloth as white as the sun.
Untying the cord that bound it, he set his beard free.

No one could take their eyes off the Cid. 3495
He approached the Counts Henry and Raymond,
gave them a big hug and begged them
to take whatever they wanted that was his.
He asked all who had taken his side 3500
to take what they pleased. Some did and others did not.

He let the king keep his two hundred marks
and take what he wished besides.
"A favor, my King, for the love of God.
Now that all this business is complete,
I kiss your hands and ask permission, lord,
to return to Valencia, which I won
with such great difficulty." 3505

[*A manuscript leaf is missing here. Menéndez Pidal has reconstructed the action from the chronicles and other accounts of the Cid:*

The Cid commanded that mounts and supplies be given to the messengers from the princes of Navarra and Aragón, and saw them on their way.

Then King Alfonso rode out, with all the highest nobles of the court, to accompany the Cid as he left town. When they reached the Zocodover, the Cid being mounted on Babieca, the king asked him, "Don Rodrigo, I've heard so much about your horse. I'd like to see you charge with him at full gallop."

The Cid gave a grin. "Lord, in your court there are many great men who'd be more than happy to do this. Ask them to play with their horses."

The king said, "I appreciate your modesty. But still, for your love of me, I'd like to see you run this horse."

The Cid urged Babieca, and ran with such speed and power that all were astonished to see his charge.]

150.

The king raised his hand and crossed himself.
"I swear by San Isidro of León,
there is no better man in all our kingdom!" 3510
The Cid rode up to him and kissed his hands.
"You asked me to run Babieca, my swift charger.
There is none like him in Moorish or Christian lands.
I give him to you as a present. Take him, lord." 3515

The king said, "I do not wish to do this.
If I did, he would not have so good a master.
A horse like this belongs with a man like you,

defeating Moors in the field and pursuing them.
God forbid that anyone should take him from you.　　　3520
From you and this horse we win honor."
With that, the court bade them farewell.

The Cid gave instructions to those about to fight.
"Now, Martín Antolínez, Pedro Vermúdez and Muño Gustióz,
be staunch in the field and bear yourselves like men.　　　3525
Let's hear good news from you in Valencia!"

Martín Antolinex replied, "Why do you say this, my lord?
We've accepted this duty, and now it's up to us.
You might hear we're dead, but not that we're defeated!"

The Cid was glad to hear this.　　　3530
Saying farewell to all his friends
the Cid headed for Valencia, the king for Carrión.

(Preparations for the Trial by
Combat)

The three weeks of grace are now complete.
The men of the Campeador arrive on time
to fulfill the duty the Cid has given them.　　　3535
They are in the care of King Alfonso.

They wait two days for the sons of Carrión.
At last they arrive with all their relatives,
well supplied with horses, arms and armor.

If they can get Rodrigo's men alone
they plan to kill them and shame the Cid.   3540
But they couldn't carry out their evil plan
because of their great fear of King Alfonso.

That night they held vigil over their arms
and prayed to the Creator.   3545

Night has passed and dawn has broken.
Many great nobles have gathered here,
eager to see the battle. Above them all
is King Alfonso, here to see justice done
and prevent any wrong.

The men of the Campeador put on their armor.   3550
All have the same thing in mind
since they all serve the same lord.
Elsewhere, the Infantes of Carrión are arming,
Count García Ordóñez giving them advice.

They brought a complaint to King Alfonso
requesting the swords Colada and Tizón   3555
not be allowed in the battle
so the Cid's men could not fight with them.
The Infantes now deeply regretted giving them back.

The king heard their plea, but would not consent.
"You had no objections when we were in court.
If you have good swords, they will serve you well.   3560
The same goes for those of the Campeador. Arise,

and take the field, Infantes of Carrión!
You must fight like men today,
for those of the Cid will not be holding back.

"If you come out well this day, you will win great honor.   3565
If you're defeated, don't blame us—
everyone knows you brought this on yourselves."

The Infantes of Carrión are now repenting,
bitterly sorry for what they've done.
They would have given all of Carrión
to call it back.   3570

When the Campeador's men were fully armed
they went to see King Alfonso.
"We kiss your hands as our King and lord.
Be faithful and fair to both them and us.   3575
Uphold us in the right, allow no wrong.

"The Infantes of Carrión have their henchmen here.
We don't know what they may have plotted.
Our lord has placed us in your hands—
do right by us, for the love of God!"   3580
The king said "With my heart and soul."

They bring out their horses, strong and fast,
make the sign of the cross on their saddles
and quickly mount.
The shields at their necks have strong bosses.
In their hands, lances with sharp steel tips.   3585

Upon each lance, a pennon fluttering.
Good men are standing all around them.

They ride out onto the field with its boundary marks.
All three of the Cid's men are agreed
that each will hit his adversary hard. 3590
On the other side are the sons of Carrión
accompanied by their numerous family.

(ALFONSO OPENS THE TRIAL. THE JUDGES
MAKE THEIR ARRANGEMENTS.)

The king appoints judges to say what is right and wrong.
No one may dispute their yes and no.
All ready on the field, Alfonso spoke: 3595

"Hear what I tell you, Infantes of Carrión!
You should have fought this battle in Toledo,
but you didn't want to have it there.
These three knights of my Cid the Campeador
I brought under my protection to Carrión.
Act lawfully, don't think of doing wrong. 3600
If anyone tries treachery, I'll stop him
and make sure he never again enjoys my kingdom!"
His words fell heavy on the sons of Carrión.

The king's judges showed them the boundary markers
and cleared the bystanders from the field. 3605
They made it clear to the six combatants

that whoever crossed the boundary line
would be considered beaten.

The onlookers stepped back, leaving a space
the length of six lances from the boundary.
The warriors drew lots for their side of the field,
arranged so the sun was equally divided. 3610
The judges withdrew from between them,
leaving the combatants face to face.

(THE COMBAT BEGINS)

The Cid's men advance on the sons of Carrión,
the Infantes upon the champions of the Cid,
each man intent upon his adversary.

They hold their shields over their hearts 3615
and lower their lances, pennons flying.
Heads bent over their saddle bows,
they put the spurs to their chargers.
The earth quakes as they reach their full gallop.
Each one is intent on the man he challenged. 3620
When the three against three collide
the onlookers fear they will all fall dead.

Pedro Vermúdez, the first to challenge his foe,
faced off against Fernando González.
They fearlessly struck each other's shields. 3625
Fernando's lance pierced Pedro's shield

but drove into nothing and never touched his flesh.
The spear shaft splintered in two places.

Pedro stayed firm and kept his balance.
He took one blow, but he struck another: 3630
breaking the boss, it shattered Fernando's shield.
Passing through the useless shield, it reached his chest.
Fernando wore three coats of mail, which saved him—
it broke through two, but lodged in the third. 3635

The blow shoved the mail,
with the shirt and quilted tunic,
a hand's breadth into the flesh.
Blood gushed from Fernando's mouth
and his cinch straps broke. He tumbled,
helpless, over the horse's rear and hit the ground. 3640

The spectators thought this wound would be his death.
Pedro Vermúdez put down his lance
and took his sword in hand.
When Fernando recognized Tizón,
before the blow could fall he said "I'm beaten."
The judges granted his plea,
and Pedro left him lying there. 3645

151.

Martín Antolínez and Diego González
charged into one another with their lances.

So bitter were the blows, both spears were broken.
Martín Antolínez laid hands on his sword,
so bright and clean it flashed across the field.
He gave Diego a glancing blow   3650
that struck off the top of his helmet.
Breaking the buckles, it cut
through his hoods of chain mail and cloth,
shaving the hair off and biting into the flesh.
Part of the helmet fell to the field,
the rest remained on his head.   3655

When the great sword Colada struck this blow
Diego could see he would not escape with his soul.
He reined his horse to turn his face away.
Martín Antolínez gave him a blow   3660
with the flat of the sword, not the edge.
Diego had a sword in hand, but did not use it.

The Infante shouted out loud "Save me God,
oh glorious Lord—and protect me from that sword!"   3665
He reined his horse away,
keeping his distance from Colada,
and rode him beyond the boundary marker.
Martín Antolínez remained on the field.

The king said, "Come, join my company.
By your deeds you have won this battle."
The judges granted that he spoke the truth.   3670

152.

Two have won victory.
I'll tell you now of Muño Gustioz
and how he got on with Ansur González.
Both struck mighty blows on the other's shield.
Ansur González, strong and brave,
broke through the shield of Muño Gustioz 3675
and pierced his armor, but failed to reach the flesh.

Returning one strike with another
Muño Gustioz shattered Ansur's shield
through the center of the boss. 3680
Ansur couldn't ward off the blow
which pierced his armor and his side,
though not his heart.
The lance head and pennon tore into flesh
and stuck out an arm's length from his back.

Giving the lance a turn, 3685
he twisted Ansur out of his saddle.
When he pulled out the lance,
the man fell onto the ground.
The shaft, the spear head and pennon
came out red. All feared that the wound was mortal.
Grasping his lance once more, Muño stands above him.
Gonzalo Ansúrez, Ansur's father, shouts
"For God's sake, don't strike! 3690
The fight is finished, and the field is won!"

The judges say "We hear you, and consent."

(The aftermath of the battle)

King Alfonso commands that the field be cleared.
The arms that are left there become his property.
The men of the Campeador depart with honor.   3695
With God's help, they were the victors in this battle.
But there is sorrow in the lands of Carrión.

The king sent my Cid's men away by night
so they would not have to fear an ambush.
Like prudent men, they rode by night and day   3700
until they reached Valencia and the Cid.
They left the Infantes of Carrión in shame,
fulfilling the duty their lord had laid upon them.
My Cid the Campeador was glad.

The Infantes of Carrión suffered deep disgrace.   3705
May whoever scorns and abandons a good woman
suffer this much, or even more!

(The Cid's honor is restored. His daughters marry into royalty.)

Let us now leave the Infantes of Carrión
to savor the bitter taste of their defeat
and speak of the man who was born in a fortunate hour.   3710

There is great rejoicing in Valencia
on account of the honor the Cid's men have won.

Their lord Ruy Díaz stroked his beard:
"Thank God in Heaven, my daughters are avenged!
Free now of their lands in Carrión, 3715
I shall marry my daughters without shame
regardless of whoever likes it or not!"

Arrangements go forward with Navarra and Aragón,
in meetings with King Alfonso of León.

The daughters are married, Doña Elvira and Doña Sol.
If the first ones were grand,
these weddings are even more magnificent 3720
and bring them greater honor than before.

See how the Cid's prestige has grown!
Now his daughters are queens of Navarra and Aragón.
Today his kinsmen are the kings of Spain 3725
and all now share in the honor of the Cid.
He passed out of time on the day of Pentecost.
May Christ grant him pardon,
and likewise us, both the sinners and the just!
These are the deeds of my Cid the Campeador
and this is the end of the story. 3730

[Addenda, by the monk who copied the manuscript:]

*To the one who wrote this book, may God grant paradise, amen!
Per Abbat wrote it in the month of May, in the year 1207.*

[Another note added at the end, apparently by a juglar, *or traveling minstrel, who may have owned this copy. This in itself is powerful evidence for public oral performances of* The Cid. *And the intended audience is obviously not learned or aristocratic, but poor and humble village peasants.]*

*The romance has been read,
now give us the wine!
If you haven't got money
then toss in some trinkets—
whatever you've got is just fine.*

Romances of The Cid

These ballads are called *romances* not because they are "romantic" but because they're composed in early Spanish, descended, along with all the Romance languages, from *Roman* Latin. Oral poetry performed to music in the marketplace, they were the popular literature of their day, as opposed to the scholarly and religious works written by monks in Latin.

One would think the short and popular ballads of the Cid were composed before the epic poem, and surely there must have been contemporary songs about him. We have a Latin *Carmen Campidoctoris*, or *Song of the Campeador*, that may have been written during his lifetime. But the *romances* of the Cid were committed to writing later than the epic poem, and some show clear signs of borrowing from it, as indeed the historical chronicles do. Perhaps these *romances* started out as popular incidents from the epic, and went on to dramatize the stories even more.

Some deal with incidents in his youth not covered by the epic. They may be based on another epic poem, *The Youthful Deeds of Rodrigo* (*Las Mocedades de Rodrigo*). Written after *The Cid*, perhaps as a sort of prequel, this poem shows a very different Rodrigo—brash, arrogant, and quick to anger. King Ferdinand calls the young Rodrigo "a raging lion." The Rodrigo of *The Cid*, in contrast, *tames* a roaring lion in his palace, taking it by the scruff of its neck and leading it back to its cage.

Though sometimes preposterous, there's no doubt these tales are entertaining. Taken all together, the romances of the Cid form a continuous narrative of his life. And though they were written down later than *The Cid*, we cannot say when they first began to circulate in oral form.

In their first printings, these romances had neither titles nor verse breaks—a typical feature of ancient poetry manuscripts. The titles and verse breaks have been added by the editor, and a few poems have been edited for length.

We begin with the most popular story of Rodrigo. This tale of the Cid's stormy courtship with Jimena appears in *The Youthful Deeds of Rodrigo*. It was picked up in the early 1600s by a Valencian dramatist, Guillén de Castro. His drama *The Youthful Deeds of the Cid*, in turn, was the basis for Pierre Corneille's world famous play *Le Cid*.

> *Rodrigo's relationship with Jimena gets off to a rocky start when he kills her father. Count Lozano insulted and struck the Cid's father, Diego Lainez, who was too old to defend himself. It fell to the Cid to defend his family's honor.*

The Cid Ponders Vengeance

The Cid was thoughtful,
considering how young he was
to be avenging his father
by killing the count Lozano.

He pondered the fearsome allies
of his powerful opponent
who had in the mountains
a thousand Austurian friends.

He considered how, in the court
of the good king Don Fernando
the Count's vote was the most important,
his arm the strongest in battle.

But all this seemed small indeed
when it came to avenging this insult,
the first shameful deed ever done
to the blood of Lain Calvo.

The Cid was not concerned
about his youth: in a noble soul
the growth of courage and valor
does not depend on years.

He took down the ancient sword
of Mudarra of Castile,
grown rusty from lack of use
after the death of its master.

"Know this, valiant sword—
that my arm is Mudarra's
and you too shall fight with his arm,
because this injury was also done to him.

"It may be that you flinch
at finding yourself in my hand,
but from now on you will not run
or take even a single step back.

"You will find me as strong as your steel
upon the field of battle.
As good as your first one was,
you have found a second master.

"And if any should conquer you,
enraged by that shameful deed
I will bury your noble blade
up to the hilt in my chest.

"To the battlefield now, for it's time
to give the count Lozano
the punishment deeply deserved
by that infamous hand and tongue."

The Cid went forth, resolute.
So determined was he, indeed
that within the space of a single hour
he had his vengeance and killed the Count.

Count Lozano: Count Gómez of Gormaz, the leading figure of King Ferdinand's court and lord of the mighty fortress of Gormaz, located near the Cid's home of Vivar. The Count is the father of Jimena Gómez, who figures in the following romances.
Laín Calvo: Ancestor of the Cid, one of the Judges who ruled Castile in its early days.
Mudarra: the man who avenged the Seven Infantes of Lara, the subjects of a lost Castilian epic. The poem implies that he was an ancestor of the Cid, who is also seeking revenge. As the name suggests, he was the son of a Christian and a Moor.

Jimena Gómez, daughter of Count Lozano, asks King Ferdinand to punish the Cid.

JIMENA DEMANDS VENGEANCE

A great clamor arose
of cries, and arms, and voices
within the palace of Burgos
where the great nobles are gathered.
The king came down from his throne
and the whole court came after him.

At the doors of the palace
they found Jimena Gómez,
her hair all disheveled,
bewailing the Count, her father—
and also Rodrigo of Vivar,
his rapier stained with blood.

They saw the angry face
the proud young man put on,
and heard what Jimena
loudly cried:

"I ask you for justice, good king
and vengeance against traitors,
so that your children may prosper
and you reap the benefits of your deeds—

for he who does not do justice
does not deserve the name of king!

"And you, cruel murderer,
don't spare me because I'm a woman.
Traitor, I ask you for death—
do not hold back or deny me—
for you have killed a gentleman,
the best among the best."

At this, when Jimena saw
that Rodrigo did not respond
but quietly taking the reins
mounted upon his horse,

turning her head to the crowd
she cried to compel them to act
and seeing they did not pursue the Cid
screamed at them, "Vengeance, my lords!"

Jimena Makes a Proposal

In Burgos the good king
was seated at his supper
when Jimena Gómez
came with her complaint.

She was dressed in mourning clothes,
all covered in black crepe.
Sinking down upon her knees
she began to speak:

"I live with a shameful stain, oh king
just like my mother.
Every day when the sun comes up
I see the man who killed my father.

"The man is mounted on his horse,
a sparrow hawk on his hand.
Adding insult to injury,
he goes to my dovecote to feed it
so that my silk blouse is stained
with the blood of my own doves.

"Do justice for me, good king!
You can't deny it to me!
A king who does not do justice
should not reign as a king

nor eat bread on a tablecloth
nor enjoy the queen."

The king, upon hearing this
began to think:
If I kill or capture the Cid
my court will revolt against me.
But if I do not do justice
God will demand it of me.

Then Doña Jimena spoke,
and her words were worthy of note:
"Now let me tell you, good king
how you can solve this problem.
You can keep your court at peace
and no one will revolt against you.

"The man who killed my father,
give him to me for my husband,
because a man who's done me such harm
I know must do me some good."

"I've always heard," Fernando said
"and now I know it's true,
that the reasoning of women
is beyond men to construe.

"Before, you demanded justice of the Cid,
and now you want to marry him!
Very well, I will send a letter
asking for him to come."

Called to court, the Cid shows his youthful temper.

THE CID FRIGHTENS FERDINAND

Diego Lainez rides
to kiss the good king's hand.
He brings three hundred
caballeros with him.

Among them was Rodrigo
the proud Castilian.
The rest are mounted on mules,
only Rodrigo is on horseback.

All are dressed in gold and silk,
only Rodrigo wears armor.
All are wearing perfumed gloves,
only Rodrigo has chain mail gauntlets.

All have girded on swords,
only Rodrigo has a golden rapier.
All are bearing poles with banners,
only Rodrigo carries a lance.

All wear richly-embroidered hats.
only Rodrigo wears a helmet
and upon that helmet a cap of red.

They ride down the road
chatting with one another
until they reach Burgos
and meet the king.

The king's companions are talking.
Some say it quietly, others aloud:
"Here he comes, among this crowd—
the one who killed Count Lozano."

When Rodrigo heard this
he fixed his gaze upon them.
In a loud voice
and proudly, he said:

"If there are any among you,
his kin or his dependants,
who are offended by his death,
come out and challenge me.

"I will defend my right
on foot or horseback, as you please."
Everyone said to themselves,
"Let the devil challenge him!"

They all dismounted
to kiss the king's hand.
Rodrigo alone
remained on his horse.

Then spoke his father,
hear what he said:
"Dismount, my son

and kiss the king's hand
for he is your lord
and you, son, are his vassal."

When Rodrigo heard this
he felt even more aggrieved.
The words he replied
were those of an angry man:

"If anyone else had said this to me,
I would have paid him back already.
But since you ask it of me, father,
I will comply willingly."

Rodrigo dismounted
to kiss the king's hand
but as he got down on his knee
his sword slipped out of its scabbard.

The king, shocked and frightened,
shouted in panic:
"Get out of here, Rodrigo!
Go! Get out of here, you devil!
You look like a man
but you act like a raging lion!"

When Rodrigo heard this
he quietly rose
and, in an altered voice
addressed the king:

"It is no honor to me
to kiss the hand of a king.
Rather, I feel offended
that my father kissed it."

With these words
he walked out of the palace.
Three hundred hidalgos
turned and went with him.

If they came here richly dressed,
they would return in armor.
If they came here riding mules,
they would return on horseback.

The next visit goes better, and Rodrigo agrees to wed Jimena.

THE WEDDING OF RODRIGO AND JIMENA

The king has pledged
his word and hand
to wed Jimena and Rodrigo
at the ancestral estate of Lain Calvo.

Love has made them forget
their old animosities
for, wherever love holds sway
quarrels and grievances fade away.

The king has granted the Cid
the towns of Valduerna and Saldana.
Belforado and San Pedro de Cardeña
have also been added to his estates.

More gallant than Gerineldos, the famous Cid
descended to the plaza
where the king, the bishop, and the nobles
stood there waiting for him.

Then Jimena descended
dressed in a ruffled gown.
Her necklace, jewels, and medallions
were worth the price of a town.

The lovers came together, gave
their hands to one another, and embraced.
The Cid, looking at his bride
spoke, deeply moved:

"I killed your father, Jimena,
but I did so with justice, not treachery.
I killed him in combat, man to man,
avenging an injury.

I killed a man and I give you a man—
here am I, at your command.
In place of the father you lost,
you have gained a husband with honor."

They do not quite live happily ever after. Jimena complains to King Ferdinand that he keeps the Cid so busy fighting she only sees him once a year. And even then he seems to suffer from what we would call PTSD—post-traumatic stress disorder.

LETTER FROM JIMENA TO THE KING

In their estate at Burgos
awaiting Rodrigo's return
Jimena is so great with child
she expects to give birth soon.

Upon a holy day
one morning, in great sorrow
bathed in tears of tenderness,
she wrote to King Fernando:

"Pardon me, my lord
but my heart is never false
and if I have a quarrel with you
I cannot conceal it.

"What law of God gives you the right,
for as long as you've been
involved in these wars,
to unmarry a married couple?

"What good reason consents
that you should only allow
my lawfully wedded husband
to visit me once a year?

"And when you do let him go
he comes home so stained with blood,
down to his horse's hoofs,
the sight of him inspires fear.

"And my arms no sooner embrace him
than he falls asleep at once
and in his dreams he thrashes and moans
as though in the throes of battle.

"And scarcely has the sun come up
than scouts and captains
are hurrying him
to return to the field again.

"If you do this to honor him,
Rodrigo has honor enough.
Still a youth without a beard,
he has Moorish kings as vassals.

"Since I have no other good
than the one that you have taken
I weep for him, although alive
as though he were dead and buried."

In another ballad, King Ferdinand replies kindly, saying Rodrigo is absent for good reason. Noting that, since she is pregnant, things may not be quite as bad as she depicts them, he offers her expected son or daughter generous presents.

The Pope and the king of France are trying to make King Ferdinand pay tribute to them. The Cid objects, and, at the Vatican, throws his most outrageous temper tantrum. Perhaps needless to say, this is a fictional—and shockingly sacrilegious— incident.

THE CID CONFRONTS THE POPE

The Pope has called
a council in Rome.
In obedience to the Pope,
King Ferdinand has come
and with him the Cid Ruy Díaz
and many great nobles as well.

Their journey done,
they dismounted at last in Rome.
The king, with great courtesy
kissed the hand of the Pope.
The Cid did not wish to do so—
he was not accustomed to kissing hands.

Rodrigo entered
the Church of St. Peter
and saw there seven thrones
belonging to the seven Christian kings.

He saw the king of France's throne
right next to the Holy Father's,

and the throne of his own king
farther away and lower down.

He strode to the king of France's throne
and knocked it over with his foot.
That throne of marble and gold
lying broken into pieces,
he took the throne of his own king
and put it in the highest place.

Then an honored duke
they called "The Savoyard" spoke:
"May you be cursed, Rodrigo
and excommunicated by the Pope,
for you have dishonored a king,
the best and most worthy of them all!"

"Forget about the kings, Duke—
they're all well and good.
Let's just the two of us
do what good vassals do."
With that he rushed at the Duke
and gave him a terrible blow.

When the Pope found out about it,
he excommunicated the Cid.
Rodrigo, on hearing this,
prostrated himself before the Pope:

"If you don't absolve me, Pope,

things will go from bad to worse—
for I will use your papal robes
as blankets for my horse!"

The Pope, the pious Father,
gave him this reply,
"I will absolve you, Don Rodrigo,
absolve you with good will,
provided you behave yourself
with greater courtesy in my court."

In the next romance, King Ferdinand has died, dividing his kingdom among his sons. War breaks out, and Sancho, the eldest, is besieging his sister Urraca in Zamora. He sends the Cid to convince her to give up the city. Urraca is outraged—and has a surprise for the Cid.

Urraca and the Cid

"Get out! Get out, Rodrigo,
you arrogant Castilian!
Do you not remember
those good times long ago

"when they knighted you
at the altar of Santiago,
when the king himself was your sponsor
and you, Rodrigo, were his godson?

"My father gave you your arms,
my mother gave you your charger,
and I strapped on your spurs of gold,
all for your greater honor.

"I thought then I would marry you.
It was not to be, for my sins!
Instead you married Jimena,
the daughter of Count Lozano.

"She may have brought you money,

but I would have brought you vast estates.
Oh, you married well, Rodrigo,
you married well indeed—
you scorned the daughter of a king
to marry the daughter of a vassal!"

When he heard this, in anguish
Rodrigo turned away.
"Out! Out, my men!
Those on foot and those on horseback!
An arrow has hit me
from that castle tower!

"Its shaft had no arrowhead of iron,
but still it has torn through my heart.
There is nothing for me now
but to live in pain forever!"

The Cid did grow up with the princess Urraca in the household of King Ferdinand. In another version we have, the Cid offers to divorce Jimena. But Urraca refuses, saying her soul would suffer. This is a good example of the process of condensation: An offer that makes us think less of the Cid has been squeezed out, so we sympathize more with his pain at the end. This romance may be from a lost epic of King Sancho.

Sancho is killed by an assassin at Zamora. His brother Alfonso succeeds to the throne. Before the Cid will kiss his hand, he makes Alfonso swear an oath that he had nothing to do with Sancho's murder.

The Oath of Santa Gadea

In Santa Gadea of Burgos
where the nobles testify,
the Cid demanded an oath
from Alfonso, the king Castile.

Taken on an iron crossbow bolt
and a crossbow made of wood,
the oath was so severe
it left the king in shock:

"May common villains kill you, king—
commoners, not nobles—
shod in coarse leather,
not in shoes with laces

"clad in peasant capes
not in fine linen or silk,
with shirts made of burlap
and not embroidered holland.

"May they be riding burros,
not mounted on mules or horses.
May their reins be of rawhide

and not tanned leather.
"May they murder you out in the wild,
not on a road or in a town,
using bone-handled knives
not golden daggers.

"May they tear out your still-beating heart
through the rib on your left-hand side
if you fail to tell the truth
about what I ask you:

"Did you take part in, or give consent
to the murder of your brother Sancho?"

The oath was so harsh
that the king was left speechless.
One of his gentlemen
whispered to him privately:

"Take the oath, good king
and don't be concerned about it.
No king can be called a traitor,
no Pope can be excommunicated."

And so the good king swore,
for he'd never found himself in such a fix.
Afterwards, deeply angered
he spoke harshly to the Cid:

"You press me hard, Rodrigo.

That was an evil oath you made me swear.
But today, although you take my oath,
afterwards you'll kiss my hand."

"I might consider it, king
if you give me a suitable gift.
Because, you know, in other lands
they'll pay for a hidalgo handsomely."

"Get out of my lands, Rodrigo!
A bad knight you've turned out to be.
And don't come back to my kingdom
until a year from this very day!"

"That's fine with me," said the Cid.
"It pleases me well
for this to be the very first thing
you've ever commanded in your kingdom.
You have exiled me for a year—
I will exile myself for four!"

The Cid has left
without kissing the hand of the king.
He has left his land in Vivar,
his homes and his estates.

The doors he left closed and bolted.
He left in their kennels
his greyhounds and hunting dogs,
taking only his falcons.

With him went three hundred
knights of noble birth,
some riding mules
others mounted on horses,

all holding lances in their fists
with tips of burnished steel,
all carrying shields
with red tassels....

We can hear some echoes here of the exile scene in the epic poem, where the doors are left ajar and the perches are empty of falcons. These are the kinds of minor variations one might expect in an oral re-creation of the epic story. Another version of this ballad has the Cid tell Alfonso "It is no honor to me / to kiss the hand of a king," the same as he did to King Fernando in an earlier ballad here. Again, this re-use of stock phrases is typical of oral composition. If we had another version of the epic poem, no doubt we'd see some interesting variations there as well.

The Cid, having won Valencia, reassures the defeated Moors that he will treat them humanely. Then he sends for his wife and daughters to join him.

THE CID SENDS FOR DOÑA XIMENA

Go then, you Moors
and bury your dead.
Care for those who are wounded,
look after the suffering.

For our ability in war
turns to humility in peace.
I do not want your homes,
I will not seize your estates.

Nor will I take your daughters
for my mistresses
for I have only one woman
and she is my natural wife.

I ask you, Alvar Fáñez
to bring from San Pedro de Cardeña
my dear wife Doña Jimena
and my two daughters with her.

Please beg of King Alfonso
to let me bring them here
and also take a present

for my natural king and lord.

And you, Martín Antolínez
go with Alvar Fáñez
and take to Raquel and Vidas,
those honorable Jews,
the three thousand marks of silver
I asked you to borrow from them.

Pay them the interest as well,
another thousand marks.
And beg them forgiveness
on my behalf

for the deception of the chests
I left them for security.
I did it because I was pressed
by my dire necessity.

And though they were distraught
that the chests were full of sand
rest assured, what was buried there
was the gold of my true word.

Here we have the resolution of the story of Raquel and Vidas, a loose end in our manuscript, but tied up neatly in the chronicles and, presumably, the versions of the epic they were based on. Martín Antolínez, "the good man of Burgos," arranged the loan in the first place.

A more admirable summary of the Cid's character could hardly be found: his kindness to Moors and Jews, his unselfishness, honor towards women, humility and loyalty, his love of his wife and family. This romance contains the essence of the man.

Before he brings Doña Jimena to Valencia, Alvar Fáñez must ask King Alfonso's permission, and present him with gifts from the Cid. The Cid's enemy at court, García Ordoñez, belittles the Cid's achievements. Alvar Fáñez, unable to bear it any longer, tells García and the king exactly what he thinks of them. His delicious tirade is reminiscent of Pedro Vermúdez's "You lie, Fernando!" at the trial—right down to the stuttering.

Alvar Fáñez speaks to the King

Alvar Fáñez arrived in Burgos
to bring the king his offering
of captives and chargers,
the riches and spoils of battle,
with the keys to a hundred towns
and castles they had conquered.

Those who saw him from afar
thought he was leading a host to battle
but fear turned to joy
when they heard the news of the Cid.

Alvar Fáñez entered the court
and begging permission
kissed the king's hand.
"Receive, your royal Highness,
from an exile nobleman
this voluntary offering.

"Of this gift he sends you
remember one thing:
it was won from the Moors
at the price of noble blood.

"In two years with his sword
the Cid has won you more land
than your father King Fernando left you,
of blessed memory.

"The Cid, who kisses your hand,
asks only one favor:
he begs that you send him
his daughters and Doña Jimena.

"Let them leave their loneliness
in San Pedro de Cardeña
and go to become the mistresses
of the city of Valencia."

Scarcely was Alvar silent
than, ready to burst with envy,
the count García Ordoñez
spoke up without courtesy:

"Don't take much account, good king,
of what the Cid has won.
For what it took him a year to gain
he could lose in a day or two.
All this stuff he's giving you

is just to make you forget his exile."
Alvar Fáñez took off his cap
and gripping it tightly in his right hand,
stuttering with furious rage,
he gave the Count this reply:

"Courtiers, slanderers—
what evil repayment you give
for the protection of his sword,
he who has so enlarged your lands!

"The Cid has won you another kingdom,
along with a hundred frontier forts—
and he wants to give you his land,
even though you threw him out of yours!

"He could have granted his land to foreigners,
but Rodrigo of Vivar,
a true Castilian by right,
would never think of doing such a thing.

"Take your ease, envious men!
Rest and relax while the Cid
stands as a fortress wall
for your lives and lands.

"Sure, spend your fortunate hours
in your palaces, at leisure—
but take better care of your honor
instead of smearing someone else's.

"And you, King, who enjoy
their flattery at your pleasure—
make yourself armies of those flatteries
and see how well they do battle!

Alvar, having "spoken truth to power" (and summed up the message of the poem) now recalls his mission for the Cid.

"Your pardon, that in my anger
I've forgotten respect for Your Highness.
Please give me, if it be your will,
the daughters and Doña Jimena.
I offer to rescue them
as though they were now in a prison."

The good King Alfonso arose
and begged Alvar Fáñez to be at ease.
The two of them, he said,
would go visit Doña Jimena together.

And then, before the entire court
he said as he paused at the door:

"I now put an end to the exile of the Cid
and give him back all of his lands.
Along with everything he has won,
I confirm his possession of Valencia

"and add to him from my own:
Ordejon, Campo, and Briviesca,

Langa and all its territories
along with the castle of Duenas.

"For the Cid's honor is mine as well,
and the honor of all of Spain."

This echoes the ending of the epic poem:
"Today his kinsmen are the kings of Spain
and all now share in the honor of the Cid."

Not all the romances show sympathy for the Moors. In this comic romance, a Moorish king imagines what he'll do when he conquers Valencia:

How the Moorish king wanted to take Valencia

Valencia, oh Valencia,
may you burn in an evil fire!
First you belonged to the Moors
and then the Christians took you.
If my lance does not lie
the Moors will win you back again.
And that dog, the Cid
I will grab by his beard
and take his wife Jimena
as my captive
and Doña Urraca, his daughter
will be my lovely mistress
and then, when I get tired of her
I'll give her to my troops!

The Cid, overhearing this, asks his daughter to flirt with the Moor, while he saddles up Babieca to chase him. Urraca, the name of King Ferdinand's daughter, may be a mistake for Elvira, the Cid's daughter in the epic.

The lovely maiden
looked out her window.

When the Moor saw her,
he said:

"May Allah guard you, mistress,
my lady Doña Urraca!"

"And you as well, my lord—
I'm so glad you could come!
For seven years now, seven
I've been in love with you."

"For just that many years, my lady,
you have been inside my soul."

While they were thus engaged
the good Cid suddenly appeared.

"Goodbye, goodbye, my lady!
Goodbye, my lovely love!
For I hear quite clearly now
the hoof beats of Babieca....

In the episode of the lion in The Cid, *the Infantes of Carrión (here called "the Counts") first show their cowardice. Diego hides behind a winepress, staining his fancy clothes. In this more comic retelling, he hides himself in a far more embarrassing place. We pick up where the lion has gotten loose:*

Fear of the Counts of Carrión

…The younger, Fernando González,
was the first to do a shameful deed:
he hid himself behind the Cid,
cowering beneath his couch.

Diego, the older of the two,
hid himself farther away
in a place so disgusting
it can't be mentioned here.

The Cid, awakened by the roaring, calmly took the lion by the scruff and put it back in its pen.

Everyone was astonished
to see such a thing, not realizing
that both of them were lions
and the Cid was the braver of the two.

Returning, then, to his room,
cheerful and not the least disturbed,

he asked about his two sons-in-law,
suspecting what had happened.

Bermudo answered:
"I'll tell you where one of them is:
he's hiding under the couch, perhaps to see
whether the lion was male or female."

Then Martín Pelaez entered,
the brave Asturian, shouting
"Good news, my lord!
they've pulled him out!"

The Cid asked, "Who?"
He replied, "The other brother,
who jumped in a place
where the Devil wouldn't swim.

"Look, my lord, he returns.
Be careful to stand far away
for if you stand next to Diego
you might need some incense to burn."

The Counts were greatly aggrieved—
from then on they hated the Cid,
wanting to turn on him, somehow
their dishonor and disgrace.

The Infantes (or Counts) ask the Cid's permission to take his daughters to Carrión. The Cid reluctantly lets them go. Once the Infantes are deep in the wilderness, they beat and abandon their wives to avenge their dishonor.

THE OAK GROVE OF CORPES

The Counts and their wives
traveling day after day
came at last to the oak grove of Corpes.
They entered a wilderness
dark and dense,
populated by towering trees.

They ordered their party
to go on ahead.
Diego, Fernando, and their wives
remained behind, alone.

The Counts dismounted
and took off their horses' reins.
When their wives saw this,
they raised a great cry.

The Counts took them off their mules
and stripped them bare.
With the reins of their horses
each one whipped his wife,
kicking them with their spurs

until they were bathed in blood.

With insults and curses
they abused the Cid's daughters.
Then the cowardly knights
abandoned them there.

"Upon you we avenge ourselves
against your father—
for you are not worthy
to marry men like us.

"Now you have paid
for the insult of the Cid
when he let the lion loose
and tried to kill us."

The account in the epic is far more graphic and detailed, and the same goes for the court scene and the trial by combat. The Cid's poet had the eye and ear of a novelist, five hundred years before the form would be invented—by another Spaniard, Miguel de Cervantes. Ironically, his Don Quixote would be making fun of the Spanish craze for romances of chivalry.

In the next romance, Jimena sends the Cid off to seek justice for their daughters. She shows herself to be a strong woman, demanding the Cid show some backbone against King Alfonso. Harking back to the beginning of the story, she is called "Jimena Gómez" here, the daughter of the Count whom the Cid killed in his youth. This sets up a cutting irony, as she calls on the Cid to be as brave as he was in avenging himself against her father.

JIMENA'S ADVICE TO THE CID

The noble Jimena Gómez
was standing by his stirrup,
speaking to the Cid
as he pulled his cloak about him.

"Remember, my lord," she said,
"your blood and that of the Count
you killed in hand to hand combat,
avenging yourself as a noble should.

"You go to the court, good Cid
where your enemies
are as cruel as they are cowardly,
as cowardly as traitors.

"They've already talked to the king
as well as their friends the Counts,
since cowards always defend themselves
with made-up stories.

"Don't take any excuses from Alfonso,
nor any of his pleas or gifts—
you can't cover up an injury
with the lipstick and rouge of reason.

"Think about your daughters
tied to two oak trees,
then demand justice from the king—
I pray to God nothing stops you."

"So it shall be, Jimena,
the famous Cid responded.
Lowering his head
he spurred Babieca and parted.

While their court and combat scenes fall short of the epic, the romances do fill out the rather sketchy ending of The Cid. After the trial by combat, Alfonso officially exiles the Infantes, who never dare show their faces again. The Cid's champions are given a grand escort home, with honors and gifts from the Cid, Jimena, and their daughters. Alfonso writes a letter to the Cid, telling him all about the combat. Perhaps other versions of the epic included some of these scenes.

The Cid's last words to his vassals, although good Christian philosophy, are especially poignant when he speaks of earthly life as an exile.

THE CID SPEAKS ON HIS DEATHBED

"I know well, my good friends
that in such a hard parting
there is no cause for joy
and much to give you pain.

But remember my words
against adverse times:
to overcome fortune means more
than conquering a thousand kingdoms.

My mother gave birth to a mortal,
and so I must die at last.
What Heaven has given as a gift
cannot be demanded as a right.

I do not die in a foreign place
but here upon my own lands—
all the more so since this earth
is the proper inheritance of the dead.

I'm not sorry to see myself die,
for if this life is an exile,
those who guide us to death
lead us back to our native land."

St. Peter appears to the Cid and promises him one last victory over the Moors—but only after his death. The bizarre scene that follows, made famous by the movie El Cid, *is not found in the epic poem as most people think, but only in the romances.*

THE CID'S FINAL BATTLE

Dead lies the good Cid,
the man from Vivar.
Gil Díaz, his vassal,
now carries out his commands.

He embalms the body,
leaving it stiff and rigid.
The face is beautiful,
its complexion rosy.

The Cid's eyes are open wide,
his beard groomed and dressed.
He did not appear to be dead,
he looks alive.

To sit him up straight
they mount the corpse on a saddle
with one board behind his back,
another in front of his chest.

His army prepared
to go out to battle

with Búcar, the king of the Moors
and all of his rabble.

When midnight came
they placed the corpse,
just as it was, on Babieca
and tied him to his horse.
He sat upright and balanced
just as he had been in life.

In his right hand
they tied his sword Tizóna.
With great ingenuity
they raised it high.

They went forth from Valencia
as day began to dawn.
Alvar Fáñez was the first
to charge out in fury
against the great host of Moors
that Búcar brought with him.

They meet a hundred Moorish Amazons, women warriors led by the beautiful Star, shooting arrows from her Turkish bow. This bit of exoticism rather backfires on the poet, however—our sympathy shifts to the Moorish women when the Christians kill them.

Búcar and his Moorish kings
stand astonished at Christian host.
Seventy thousand knights at least,

all white as snow, they seem.
One above all amazes them,
a figure greater than the rest.
On a white charger he is mounted
with a red cross on his chest.

In his upraised fist
a bright beacon gleams—
a sword flashing fire,
signaling destruction for the Moors.

The Moors are slaughtered and flee, in a replay of the battle with Búcar in The Cid. In actual history, King Alfonso, knowing he couldn't hold Valencia after the death of the Cid, takes Ximena and Rodrigo's vassals back to Castile. They bury the Cid at San Pedro de Cardeña, where his tomb, and Ximena's, can still be seen. This romance also ends there, with a line that echoes the ending of the epic poem:

Now they head back to Castile
as the good Cid commanded.
They have arrived
at San Pedro of Cardeña.
There rests the body of the Cid
who won so much honor for Spain.

The *Carmen Campidoctoris*

The Latin *Carmen Campidoctoris* may have been written during the lifetime of the Cid. This unfinished poem was discovered in a monastery in Catalonia. The Cid did spend some time in Catalonia, at the court of the Count of Barcelona, during his first exile. The Cid left in a huff, apparently over some insult, and later defeated the Count in battle.

This Count, named Berenguer Ramón, was suspected of killing his co-ruler and twin brother, named Ramón Berenguer (*The Cid*, understandably, confuses the two). The Church was very unhappy with "The Fratricide," as he was known, and in fact a civil war was launched against him.

This poem may have been written not only to praise the Cid, also but to attack Berenguer. The monastery in which the manuscript was found had once been under his brother's rule. The Count certainly looks bad, even ludicrous, in *The Cid*, and perhaps in the missing ending of this poem.

The poem is a product of writing rather than oral composition. It's in literary Latin, with learned classical allusions. Its verse form is tight and demanding, with regular stanzas, unlike *The Cid*'s loose and rambling lines. It seems to be introducing the Cid to a Catalan audience which might not have known much about him. The fragment we have ends, somewhat suspiciously, with a buildup to the battle between the Cid and the Count of Barcelona.

CARMEN CAMPIDOCTORIS
(SONG OF THE CAMPEADOR)

We could sing of the famous deeds
of Paris, Pyrrhus[1], and Aeneas,
praised so often and so highly
by so many poets.

But what good are those pagan fables,
so old now they're just clichés?
Of Rodrigo, the Prince of Battles,
let us sing today.

A thousand books could never hold
his numerous victories.
Not even Homer himself,
with all his strength, could sing them all.

Still I, with little learning,
having heard but a fraction of his deeds
will, like a fearful mariner,
raise my poetic sail into the wind.

Lo! Let all people listen with delight
to the song of the Campeador!
Most of all those who rely on his strength,
gather round!

---

[1] see notes on p. 241

He was born of a noble stock—
there is none better in Castile. 2
Seville and the banks of the Ebro
also know Rodrigo well.

In his first single combat as a youth
he defeated a knight from Navarre.
Henceforth the name of "Campeador"
would be on the lips of all great men.

He gave promise of great deeds already,
how he would overcome Counts in battle,
crushing royal armies underfoot,
subduing them with his sword.

King Sancho so delighted in the youth,
seeing him scale such heights,
that he gave Rodrigo command
over all his kingdom's troops.

Rodrigo was reluctant to accept, but Sancho
would have granted him even higher honors
had he not so suddenly met with death,
which spares no man.

After the treacherous murder of Sancho,
King Alfonso gained the throne
and, as his brother promised,
inherited all of Castile.

Alfonso soon loved the Campeador[3] no less,
and began to exalt him above the rest
so that his peers at the palace
began to envy Rodrigo.

"My lord, what are you doing?"
they asked the king. "You're just making
trouble for yourself. To raise Rodrigo
to such heights displeases us.

"Mark our words: he will never love you,
for he was a member of your brother's court.
He will always be plotting and planning
some evil against you."

Hearing their whispered words,
Alfonso's heart was seized with suspicion,
fearing the loss of his honors
and his throne.

All his love now turned to wrath.
He looked for chances to accuse Rodrigo,
in matters of which he knew little
and was ignorant of much.

He exiled the man from his land.
From that moment onward, Rodrigo
began to make war on the Moors,
devastating Spanish lands and sacking cities.

A rumor arrived at the court
that the Campeador and the leading Hagarites[4]
were preparing a fatal trap
for Alfonso and his men.

Furious, Alfonso gathered his cavalry,
planning to kill him if he was unwary,
commanding that, if the Campeador were captured,
his throat should be cut.

The king sent the proud, famous Count García
to fight against Rodrigo,
but the Campeador won the field,
defeating García yet again.

This was the second battle in which García
was taken prisoner, with many others.
Rodrigo had also captured his camp
at a place called Cabra.[5]

And so through every part of Spain
his name is known to all the kings
who equally fear the Campeador
and pay him tribute.

A third battle he fought
where God granted him victory,
subduing some, putting others to flight,
and capturing their camp.

Then the Marquis, Count of Barcelona
to whom the Midianites pay tribute
joined with Al Fagib of Lerida
and his Moorish hosts.

They surrounded the castle of Caesar Augustus [6]
which the Moors today call Almenara.
Rodrigo asked them to grant him a truce
so he could send for help.

Since they denied his request
and refused to grant him free passage,
he commanded his men to arm themselves
without a moment's delay.

He was the first to put on his chain mail shirt—
no man ever saw a better one—
and strap on his sword, adorned with gold
by a master hand. [7]

He took up his lance of wondrous make
hewn from the ash tree of a noble forest,
its hard straight iron point, by his order
whetted sharp.

On his left arm he bore a shield
all chased in gold
on which a fierce dragon
was brilliantly painted.

Protecting his head was a gleaming helmet
decorated with silver plates
and fitted with bands of electrum
all around.

He mounted a horse a barbarian brought
from across the sea. He wouldn't have sold it
for a thousand gold coins, for it ran faster
than the wind, jumped higher than a deer.

Armed and mounted in such splendor,
not Paris nor Hector in the Trojan War
could have excelled him,
nor were any in our times his equal.

Then he prayed....

(Ten verses at the end were scraped off the parchment of the manuscript. Were they erased to hide their attack on Berenguer Ramón? The Count survived the civil war against him, and likely would not have been pleased to see this poem.)

Notes to *Carmen Campidoctoris*

1. Pyrrhus: a Greek general who defeated the Romans in one engagement, but lost so many men he could not continue the war. According to Plutarch, he said "If we are victorious in one more battle with the Romans, we shall be utterly ruined." Hence the ironic phrase "Pyrrhic victory." (p. 235)

2. "noble stock, none better in Castile": None better, perhaps, but some, like Count García Ordoñez, had much nobler titles. (p. 236)

3. Campeador: another honorary title for Rodrigo, meaning "champion, victor in battle." The Latin Campidoctoris literally meant "master of the field," a role he filled for Sancho as the master and leader of his army in the field. The title of "Cid" is never used here; perhaps he had not acquired it yet. He fought the knight from Navarre as King Sancho's champion in judicial combat, to resolve a land dispute. (p. 236)

4. Hagarites (and later Midianites): The Arabs, supposedly descended from Abraham's second wife Hagar. (p. 238)

5. Cabra, García Ordoñez: The Cid's first victory against Ordóñez was at the Battle of Cabra, during his tribute mission to Seville. The second came when Alfonso tried to take Valencia from the Cid. The campaign was aborted, sparing the Cid from fighting Alfonso directly. Instead, he retaliated by ravaging García's lands. He and García agreed to meet for a battle, but García never appeared. (p. 238)

6. Caesar Augustus: The original Roman name for

Saragossa or Zaragoza, a Moorish kingdom the Cid was helping during his first exile. It was proper siege "etiquette" to allow a town to send for help, on condition that it would surrender if no help came within a given time. (p. 239)

7   This scene of the Cid arming himself reminds one of the elaborate dressing scene before the court in Toledo. In both cases it is the prelude to a major climax of the poem. His shield really did have a dragon on it. Electrum is an alloy of gold and silver. The Cid's famous horse, Babieca, was won in battle with the Moors. (p. 239)

Selected Readings

Spanish text of *The Cid*

Anonymous. *Cantar de Mio Cid*, edited with studies by Alberto Montaner, Real Academia Española; Galaxia Gutenberg, 2011.

———. *Poema de Mio Cid*, edited with notes and introduction by Ramón Menéndez Pidal, *Clásicos Castellanos* edition; Madrid: Espasa-Calpe, S. A., 1963. Together with *La España del Cid* (below), Menéndez Pidal's work is the essential starting point for discussions about *The Cid*.

English translations

Raffel, Burton. *The Song of The Cid*. Penguin Classics, 2009. A readable but rather loose translation of *The Cid*. Introduction and notes by Maria Rosa Menocal (see her book below).

Hamilton, Rita, and Janet Perry. *The Poem of the Cid*. Manchester U. Press, 1975; Penguin Books, 1984. Prose translation, based on the manuscript research of Ian Michael.

Merwin, W. S.. *Poem of the Cid*. New American Library, 1959. This verse translation is by one of America's finest poets, but its language and word order seem stilted at times.

History and Criticism

Menéndez Pidal, Ramón. *La España del Cid*. Madrid: Espasa-Calpe, S. A., 1967.

_____. *The Cid and his Spain*, translated by Harold Sunderland, London: John Murray, 1934. A treasure trove of historical detail and fascinating insights about the period and the Cid.

Fletcher, Richard. *The Quest for El Cid*. Oxford U. Press, 1991.

_____. *Moorish Spain*. Henry Holt and Company, 1992.

Barton, Simon, and Richard Fletcher. *The World of El Cid: Chronicles of the Spanish Reconquest*. Manchester U. Press, 2000.

Harney, Michael. *The Epic of The Cid, with Related Texts*. Hackett, 2011.

Martínez Diez, Gonzalo. *El Cid Histórico*. Barcelona: Planeta, 2016. (Spanish)

Rosa Menocal, María. *The Ornament of the World*. New York: Back Bay Books, 2003. Charming study of the coexistence and interaction of Muslims, Jews, and Christians in Muslim Spain.

Literary works about the Cid

Romances

Romancero del Cid, edited by F. S. R., Collección Crisol Núm. 41; Madrid: Aguilar S. A., 1951 (Spanish)

Flor Nueva de Romances Viejos, edited by Ramón Menéndez Pidal, Austral; Espasa Libros, 2012. (Spanish)

El Romancero, edited by Conrado Guardiola Alcover, Clásicos Ebro; Zaragoza: Editorial Ebro, S. L., 1973. (Spanish)

Cancionero de Romances Viejos, edited by Margit Frenk Alatorre, México: UNAM Press, 1961. (Spanish)

Spanish Traditional Ballads, translated by Stanley Appelbaum, Dover, 2003. (Dual language)

Spanish Ballads, translated by W. S. Merwin, Copper Canyon, 2008. Reprint of a 1961 edition. (English only)

Longer Poems

Anonymous. *'Carmen Campidoctoris' o Poema Latino del Campeador*. Edited by Alberto Mantaner and Ángel Escobar. Madrid: Espana Nuevo Milenio, 2001.

Anonymous. *Las Mocedades de Rodrigo: The Youthful Deeds of Rodrigo, the Cid*, edited and translated by Matthew Bailey. Medieval Academy Books No. 110; U. of Toronto Press, 2007. This short epic contains popular stories about the young Cid. Probably written around 1300, the surviving manuscript seems to be drawn from both historical documents and unhistorical romances, with little sense of style or continuity. Valuable for literary historians.

Plays

de Castro, Guillén. *Las Mocedades del Cid*. Madrid: Espasa-Calpe, 1981. Excellent theatrical treatment by Guillén de Castro (1569-1631) based on the romances and perhaps *Las Mocedades de Rodrigo* (see above). (Spanish)

Corneille, Pierre. *Le Cid*, translated by John C. Lapp. Crofts Classics, AHM Publishing, 1955.

_____. *The Cid, Cinna, the Theatrical Illusion*, translated by John Cairncross. Penguin Books, 1975. Corneille's world-famous play was adapted from Guillén de Castro's (see above). Both deal with the star-crossed love of Rodrigo and Jimena Gómez, found in the romances but not in *The Cid* itself.

www.ingramcontent.com/pod-product-compliance
Lightning Source LLC
Chambersburg PA
CBHW021357290426
44108CB00010B/282